Small Town
MISSOURI

Legends, Lore, and Attractions in the Show Me State

Caitlin Yager

Copyright © 2025, Reedy Press, LLC
All rights reserved.

Reedy Press
PO Box 5131
St. Louis, MO 63139
reedypress.com

No part of this publication may be reproduced or transmitted in any form or by any means, electronic or mechanical, including photocopy, recording, or any information storage and retrieval system, without permission in writing from the publisher. Permissions may be sought directly from Reedy Press at the above mailing address or via our website at reedypress.com.

Unless otherwise noted, all photos are courtesy of the author or believed to be in the public domain.

Library of Congress Control Number: 2024949386

ISBN: 9781681065861

25 26 27 28 29   5 4 3 2 1

Please note that websites, phone numbers, addresses, and business names are subject to change. We did our best to relay the most accurate information available, but due to circumstances beyond our control, please do not hold us liable for misinformation. When exploring new destinations, please do your homework before you go.

CONTENTS

INTRODUCTION	1
ARROW ROCK	3
AUGUSTA	6
BETHEL	8
BLACKWATER	10
BOONVILLE	13
BOURBON	16
BUTLER	18
CALEDONIA	20
CAMERON	22
CARL JUNCTION	24
CARROLLTON	26
CHILLICOTHE	28
CUBA	31
DEFIANCE	34
DONIPHAN	37
EMINENCE	40
EXCELSIOR SPRINGS	43
FULTON	46
GLASGOW	48
HAMILTON	50
HANNIBAL	52
HERMANN	55
JACKSON	58
JAMESPORT	60
KEYTESVILLE	62
KIMMSWICK	65
KIRKSVILLE	68
LAMAR	70
LEXINGTON	73
LOUISIANA	76
MANSFIELD	78
MARCELINE	80
MARSHFIELD	82
MARTHASVILLE	85
MEXICO	89
NEOSHO	92
NEW HAVEN	94
PACIFIC	97
PERRYVILLE	101
PIEDMONT	104
ROCHEPORT	107
SALEM	110
SEDALIA	113
ST. JAMES	117
STE. GENEVIEVE	120
STEELVILLE	124
VAN BUREN	126
WAYNESVILLE	128
WESTON	131
WESTPHALIA	134
SOURCES	136
INDEX	139

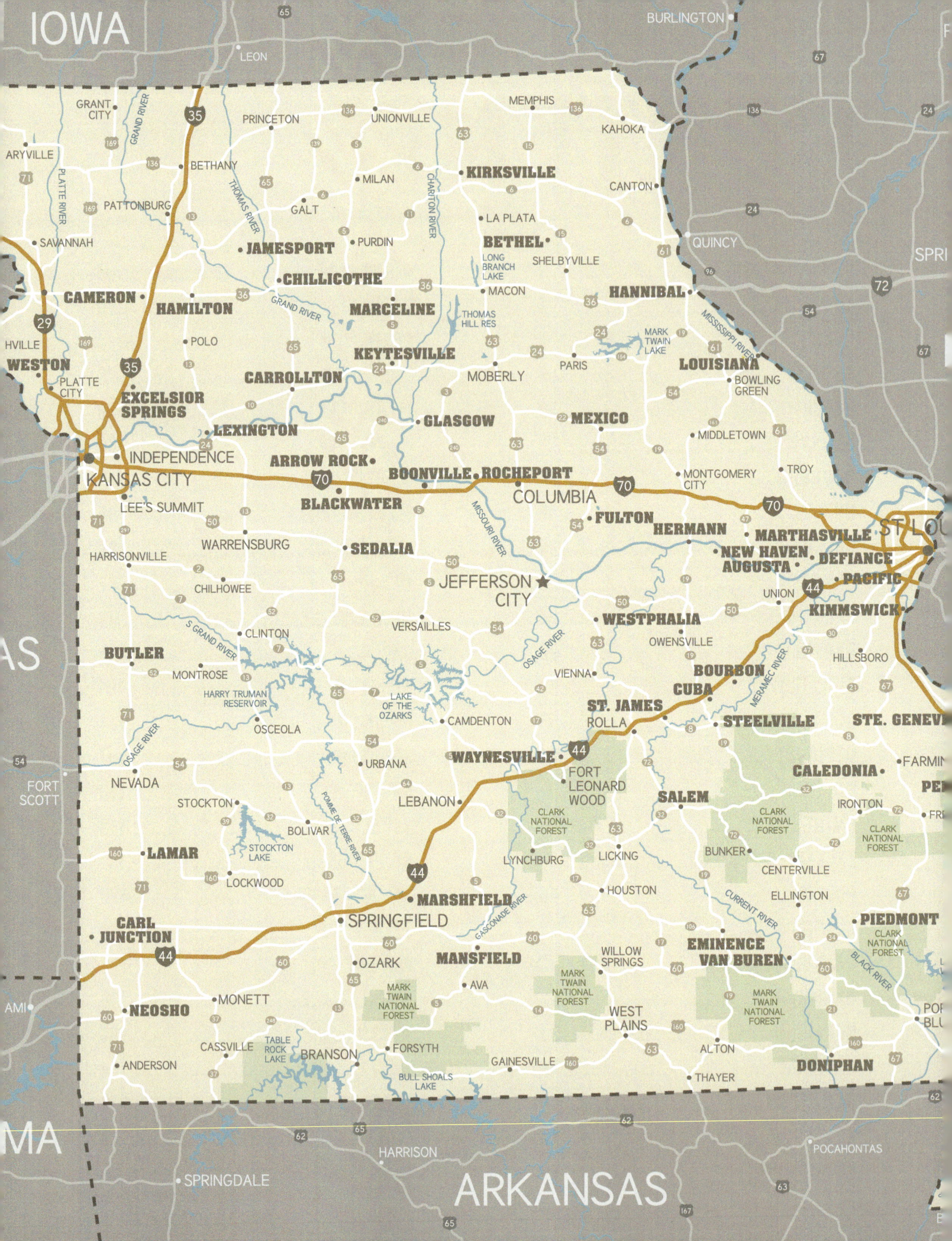

INTRODUCTION

While Missouri is known to most as the home of the Mizzou Tigers, Kansas City Chiefs, St. Louis Cardinals, and other bigger city attractions, it's the areas in between that help tell the full story of Missouri's culture, heritage, and people. Nestled among rolling hills, scenic rivers, and vast farmland are hundreds of small towns with fascinating stories and places. Highlighted in the following pages are 50 Missouri small towns, all with unique sites to visit, intriguing histories to explore, and sprawling natural beauty. Hop in the car, purchase a train ticket, or jump on your bike to set out on an adventure to discover the wonder and awe of small town Missouri.

Round Spring Cave in Eminence
Courtesy of See the Ozarks

The Lyceum Theatre puts on performances throughout the year.
Courtesy of Ryan J. Zirngibl

ARROW ROCK

Saline County — Population 59

Founding Story

If you're looking for small town charm, beautiful natural scenery, and fascinating history, look no further than the town of Arrow Rock—the smallest of our featured communities with a population of only 59 people. The "Arrow Rock" bluff—first noted on a 1732 French map as "pierre a fleche" or "rock of arrows"—was a significant point for Indigenous peoples along the Missouri River and eventually explorers and westward travelers. Arrow Rock is part of what was named "Boone's Lick Country," named for a well-known salt lick across the river.

During the early 19th century, the area saw steady migration from European immigrants in states like Kentucky, Tennessee, and Virginia, and travelers moved through along the Santa Fe Trail. At its founding in 1829, this mid-Missouri town was called "Philadelphia," but the name was changed to honor the well-known "Arrow Rock" landmark. Steamboats on the Missouri River helped the community thrive as a river port in the mid- to late 19th century, and Arrow Rock reached its peak population of 1,000 people by the start of the Civil War.

Its location in a war-torn state like Missouri during and after the Civil War led the community to experience significant economic turmoil, and the population saw steep decline as the town was bypassed during the railroad boom. However, Arrow Rock's significant 19th-century architecture soon attracted visitors, inspiring the establishment of the Friends of Arrow Rock in 1959. The organization is a nonprofit preservation organization that has helped make Arrow Rock a true case study in cultural heritage preservation and tourism, so much so that the whole town was named a National Historic Landmark in 1963. Of note is the preservation of the J. Huston Tavern, which opened in 1834 and is one of the oldest continuously operated restaurants west of the Mississippi. In addition to the restaurant, visitors can view the historic kitchen and upstairs furnishings.

Today, the Friends of Arrow Rock has over 800 members for this tiny town of under 100 residents, and they've all helped Arrow Rock become renowned across the country for its historic buildings, entertainment venues, natural beauty, and antique shops. Start your Arrow Rock adventure at the Arrow Rock State Historic Site's visitor center, which is home to over 9,000 square feet of exhibits featuring an impressive artifact collection.

Missouri artist George Caleb Bingham
Courtesy of the St. Louis Art Museum

Legends

Missouri artist George Caleb Bingham has deep roots in this town, and he built his first home in Arrow Rock in 1837. Though the renowned artist would travel all across the United States and Europe in his lifetime, Arrow Rock was home, and his house is now listed on the National Register of Historic Places and included in the Arrow Rock State Historic Site.

Lore

Archaeological evidence shows that for nearly 12,000 years, Indigenous peoples in the area used Arrow Rock bluff as a manufacturing site for flint tools and weapons, which is how the bluff—and later the town—got its name.

The J. Huston Tavern is the oldest continuously operating restaurant west of the Mississippi.
Courtesy of the Library of Congress

Attractions

Check out the George Caleb Bingham House, performances at the Lyceum Theatre, and the J. Huston Tavern (the oldest continuously operating restaurant west of the Mississippi); tour exhibits at the Visitor Center; and be sure to visit the Old Courthouse and African American Experience Museum.

Events

One of Arrow Rock's biggest draws is performances at the renowned Lyceum Theatre. It also hosts an annual Heritage Festival, which has been held for over 50 years, and nothing beats Old Fashioned Christmas in the Village during the holidays.

Vitals / Fun Facts

- The town's eventual name was first seen on a 1732 French map, called "pierre a fleche." This literally translates to "rock of arrows."
- The town of Arrow Rock is designated as a National Historic Landmark for its rich history and cultural heritage.

African American Experience Museum
Courtesy of Friends of Arrow Rock

Arrow Rock's museums share the area's history.
Courtesy of Friends of Arrow Rock

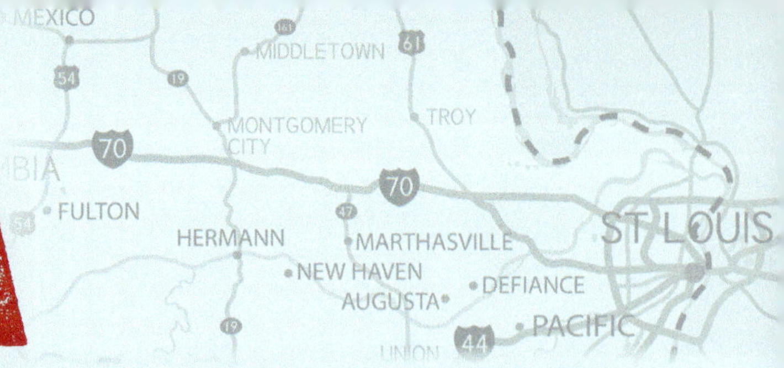

AUGUSTA

St. Charles County — POPULATION 270

Founding Story

Missouri wine country enthusiasts may know all about Augusta, but this little town in St. Charles County is so much more than wine. Augusta, like many communities in this region of Missouri, was founded in the mid-19th century by German immigrants, though it went by a different name at first. The town was called "Mount Pleasant" when registered in 1836, but another town of the same name, combined with the growing population of Missouri, created the need for a new town name. However, the reasoning for the choosing of "Augusta" is apparently unknown. The town's early growth was largely due to its location on the Missouri River, an asset for merchants and other business owners, but flooding caused the Missouri River to move in the 1870s, and Augusta was no longer on the river. However, this left large amounts of very fertile river bottom land, which aided in establishing a prosperous agricultural industry. Though the wine industry was badly hurt during Prohibition, the Augusta area saw revival in its wineries in the 1960s. Today, Augusta is a destination for anyone looking for stunning hills and valleys, award-winning wine, quaint B&Bs, and unique shops.

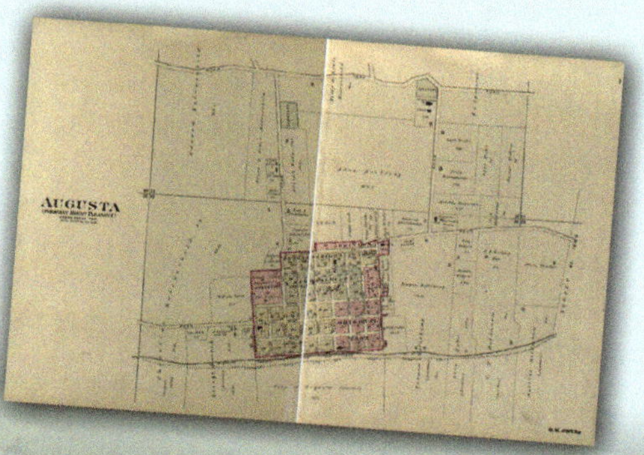

Sunflower Hill Farm grows much of its own food for its restaurant and provides stunning views from its patio.
Courtesy of Sunflower Hill Farm

Augusta Map
Courtesy of the State Historical Society of Missouri

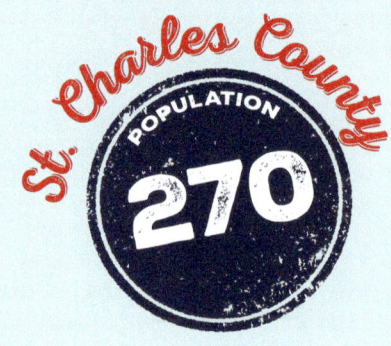

6 | SMALL TOWN MISSOURI

Legends
Anita Mallinckrodt, local author and town historian, was known throughout Missouri for her expertise on St. Charles and Warren County history. Her German family had deep roots in the Augusta area, and Mallinckrodt wrote many books on the story of German people and heritage in Missouri, as well as general history of the towns.

Lore
Missouri has become an attractive tourist center for the wineries, but did you know Missouri viticulture saved the wine industry in France? In the 1870s, an infestation wiped out nearly half of France's vineyards. At this time, winemaking was taking off in this area of Missouri, and vintners here sent root stock from their grape crops to France to help restore their vineyards.

Attractions
Be sure to visit the Augusta Harmonie Verein for a bit of history and regular live music and events. Carve out time to walk the historic downtown and visit the unique shops and buildings. Make reservations for a date night at the renowned Root restaurant or spend a beautiful day at the wineries. If outdoor recreation is more your style, hop on the Katy Trail or explore nearby Klondike Park.

Events
Augusta is known throughout the country for its annual Plein Air Festival, and there are regular live music and cultural events at the historic Augusta Harmonie Verein building.

Vitals / Fun Facts
- Augusta was honored as the first American Viticulture Area in 1980.
- The Augusta Harmonie Verein was built in 1869 and originally served as a clubhouse of sorts for the local German population.

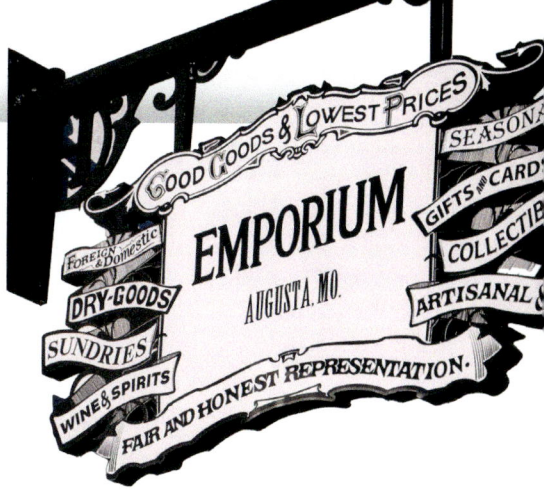
Downtown Augusta offers shopping, restaurants, and historic buildings.
Courtesy of Visit Augusta Missouri

Because of its wine heritage, Augusta was named the first American Viticulture Area in the 1980s.
Courtesy of Visit Augusta Missouri

German immigrants felt at home at the Augusta Harmonie Verein, a cultural and social club for the area.

The gazebo at the Augusta Harmonie Verein overlooks the stunning Missouri River Valley.

BETHEL

Shelby County
POPULATION
135

Founding Story

If you're on the hunt for a small town experience rooted in an intriguing past, head to Bethel, Missouri! Bethel is a bit different from the other towns in this book; it's a community founded in 1844 as a religious communal colony by a German man named Wilhelm Keil and his followers. Though there was no formal agreement for the society, and residents were allowed to earn their own money, they did share labor and property with one another. For several decades, the commune thrived until Keil and a handful of followers decided to journey west. The communal society was disbanded between 1879 and 1881, but Bethel remained a small community with residents, active businesses, and community gatherings. Most notably, Bethel was known for its musicians and artisans, a heritage still seen in the community today. Today, Bethel's story is preserved in many original buildings and in town festivals, and the community is still a thriving small town dedicated to preserving its fascinating history.

Several of the colony's original structures have been preserved.
Courtesy of Historic Bethel German Colony

Legends
Henry Theophilus Finck was a prolific music editor and critic with the *New York Evening Post* during what many refer to as the Golden Age of Music in the late 19th century and into the early 20th century. Finck was born in Bethel, and he and his family sold instruments to the many musicians in town, but the Fincks were not officially members of the communal society. However, the family did follow Keil and his colonists to Aurora.

Lore
Wilhelm Keil, born in Prussia in 1812, came to America and in 1844 established a communal society in Bethel. After about 10 years in Bethel, Keil worried the commune was too susceptible to influence from a rapidly growing Missouri. He and a group of followers headed west on the Oregon Trail, never to return to Missouri, though the Bethel commune continued for about 20 more years. Out west, Keil founded one of the most successful utopian community experiments west of the Rocky Mountains—the Aurora Colony in Oregon.

Attractions
The Historic Bethel German Colony's preserved structures from the days of the commune are there to represent the community's history. Be sure to come visit in April for the Bethel Colony Spring Market.

Events
Bethel hosts a popular Fiddle Camp each year, in addition to seasonal markets and a Christmas in Bethel event.

Vitals / Fun Facts
- During its prime, the Bethel colony and its residents were known for their music and handcrafted goods, which inspire the fiddle camp and markets.

Members of Bethel's German Communal Society made their own musical instruments, a tradition the town honors to this day.
Courtesy of Rural Missouri

Bethel was first settled by a group of Germans led by Wilhelm Keil, who formed a religious communal colony in 1844.
Courtesy of Historic Bethel German Colony

Bethel's museum preserves and shares the stories of this unique community.
Courtesy of Historic Bethel German Colony

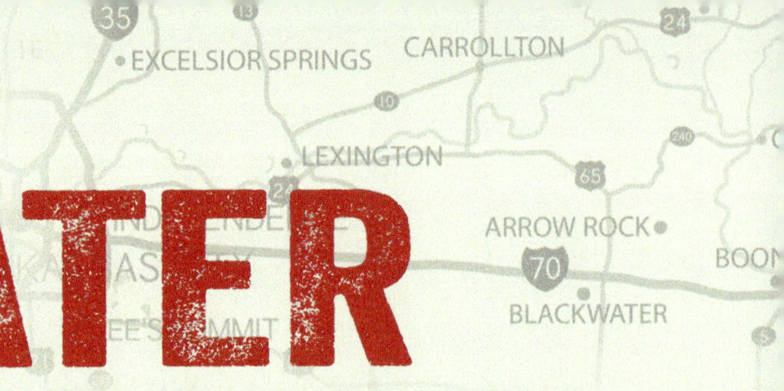

BLACKWATER

Cooper County
POPULATION 173

Beautiful Blackwater, Missouri, is steeped in history, charm, and natural splendor. The town is located just off of one of Missouri's main thoroughfares, Interstate 70, about 40 minutes west of Columbia, but the community has stayed true to its small town roots. Missouri's growth skyrocketed as railroads became more in-demand, and many Missouri communities owe their founding and growth to one of the many railroads that came through Missouri in the second half of the 19th century. In this case, Blackwater was founded in 1887 to service the Missouri-Pacific Railroad. The community was situated along the railroad's "River Route," a vastly important rail line that connected Kansas City, Boonville, and Jefferson City, among others, keeping the town busy and relevant during the height of the railroad era. Though quite small in population, this community is full of activity and is listed on the National Register of Historic Places.

Visitors to Blackwater find the town's ambiance nostalgic.
Courtesy of City of Blackwater

Blackwater's downtown main street is picturesque with historic buildings and local businesses.
Courtesy of City of Blackwater

10 | SMALL TOWN MISSOURI

Legends

An archaeological site in the area found by J. Mett Shippee is dated to the Middle Woodland Period (about 200 BCE to 500 CE) and is attributed to Hopewell culture. Obsidian found at the site can be traced to the obsidian cliff in Yellowstone National Park.

Lore

The town is named for the river, which is believed to have been named by Native Americans, because of the rich, black soil in the river bottoms.

The Blackwater Depot has been preserved and maintained to honor the community's railroad heritage.
Courtesy of Morgan Lee Photography

Attractions

For the history lover, visit the Iron Horse Hotel (built in 1889 and originally the "Frady Hotel"), the Blackwater Depot, and the Telephone Museum. Shop local goods at the Morning Glory Farms store, perk up at River & Rail Coffee, find some treasure at Prairie Lawn School Antiques, or enjoy a performance at the historic West End Theatre.

Telephone Museum
Courtesy of Blackwater Preservation Society

Events

The town hosts two annual festivals, the Blackwater Spring Festival and the Blackwater Fall Festival. It also welcomes visitors to its Ice Cream Stroll in the summer and Christmas Market during the holidays.

Vitals/Fun Facts

- You've heard of a "one-light town" as a way to describe how small a town is . . . but Blackwater is a "no-light" town. There are no stoplights in this community.

Blackwater Windmill
Courtesy of Central MIssouri Loop

Hotel Frederick is one of more than 400 sites in town listed on the National Register of Historic Places.
Courtesy of Hotel Frederick

BOONVILLE

Founding Story

Boonville is a history-lover's paradise, with over 400 sites listed on the National Register of Historic Places throughout town. There's no shortage of unique stories, people, and places to explore in this bustling river community. Boonville and the surrounding area were known as "Boonslick" in its early days of settlement, the name hailing from a saltlick found nearby by Daniel Boone's sons, Nathan and Daniel Morgan, in the early 1800s. Salt was a valuable mineral at the time, needed for preserving food and tanning hides, and the Boones would boil the spring water to extract the salt.

Platted in 1817, the town prospered throughout the first part of the 19th century as a trade point on the Missouri River and on the Santa Fe Trail, and was officially incorporated in 1839. Boonville's location made it a sought-after target for both Union and Confederate forces during the Civil War. As a result, the town and the surrounding area were the sites of multiple battles and occupations, causing significant stress for the once thriving and progressive community. Thespian Hall, a still popular historic site in town, was even used as a hospital and morgue during those trying times. However, a decisive victory during the first battle in Boonville secured and kept the Missouri River for the North for the remainder of the war.

The town's location on the railroad helped its continued growth, and Boonville remained a major transportation hub throughout the 19th and 20th centuries. A large railroad depot was built in the 1910s, eventually seeing up to 30 trains come through each day. The depot still stands and has been meticulously restored, now used by the Boonville Chamber of Commerce. Several other institutions contributed to Boonville's community and economic growth, such as Kemper Military School (the oldest military school west of the Mississippi) and Thespian Hall. With the development of the Katy Trail in the 1990s, interest in Boonville as a tourism attraction grew, and the town has become a popular stop as a picturesque river community with a beautiful downtown.

Cooper County
POPULATION 7,964

Thespian Hall at Fifth and Vine Streets
Courtesy of the Library of Congress

Nathan Boone
Courtesy of the State Historical Society of Missouri

Legends

Nathan and Daniel Morgan, Daniel Boone's sons, established the salt-making operation in the area, and the trail they forged from St. Charles to what became Howard County inspired the "Boonslick" moniker used to name the Boonslick Trail and to reference the area.

Lore

The Old Cooper County Jail and Hanging Barn was the site of the last public hanging in the state in 1930, and was also the longest operating jail in Missouri, from 1848 to 1979. Frank James, brother of the infamous Jesse James, was jailed there for a time.

Attractions

The Katy Trail and Boonville's historic Katy Depot are popular town draws. Visit Warm Springs Ranch to see where the Budweiser Clydesdales reside, or if history is more your interest, head to the River, Rails & Trails Museum; Mitchell Antique Motorcar Museum; and Old Jail and Hanging Barn.

The Katy Depot is the last of five Spanish Mission–style depots standing along the MKT Railroad/Katy Trail.

Events

For lovers of music, history, arts, and more, make plans to visit Boonville's Big Muddy Folk Festival, Heritage Days, Festival of the Arts, or Steam Engine Festival. Also check out the Pedaler's Jamboree on the Katy Trail, a combination biking and music festival.

Vitals / Fun Facts

- Boonville has more than 400 sites in town listed on the National Register of Historic Places.
- Of the five Spanish Mission-style depots built along the Missouri, Kansas, Texas Railroad (also known as the "MKT" or "Katy") Boonville's depot is the last standing.
- Thespian Hall is an eyewitness to many years of Boonville history as the longest continuously operating theater west of the Allegheny Mountains. The hall was also used as a hospital and morgue during the Civil War, and tours of Thespian Hall are available by appointment.

Boonville's section of the Katy Trail provides a scenic ride through cool shade.

What once housed a wholesale grocer is now home to the Boonville Visitors Center, just steps from the Katy Trail.
Courtesy of Boonville Tourism

Boonville Bridge over the Missouri River
Courtesy of Boonville Tourism

BOURBON

Crawford County
POPULATION
1,528

Founding Story

Nestled in the lush, scenic Missouri Ozark foothills is the town of Bourbon. The Missouri Pacific Railroad inspired the town's establishment in the 1850s during heightened interest in westward expansion, though the town wasn't officially incorporated until decades later in 1907. The railroad attracted workers to the community, many of which were Irish immigrants. The Irish townsfolk helped inspire the town's name, as the men would gather at the general store and enjoy bourbon whiskey together after their workday. Over the next few decades, the fertile and widely available land intrigued farmers and ranchers, who began to settle the area and grow their industries. The town continued to expand as Route 66 came through Bourbon in the 1920s, a catalyst for economic growth and launching the town into a new era. Steady growth continued for about 30 years, until the new four-lane alignment of Route 66 bypassed Bourbon's business district. Today, Bourbon has a variety of interesting sites to experience, beautiful scenery, and outdoor recreation, as well as its original water tower right on the highway beckoning visitors to come explore.

Barrels labeled "Bourbon" throughout town are both an homage to the community's history and markers for the Barrel Tour.
Courtesy of Bourbon, MO

Bourbon has become a destination for floating.
Courtesy of Blue Springs Ranch

Attractions

Bourbon is surrounded by wonderful outdoor recreation options, including Blue Springs Creek Conservation Area; Blue Springs Ranch for camping and floating along the Meramec River; and Onondaga Cave State Park, a National Natural Landmark and home to some of the most picturesque "show caves" in the country. For stunning panoramic views, visit Vilander Bluff Natural Area.

Events

Head to Bourbon for its fall festival, car show, live music, farm tours, and seasonal events at Heartland Farms, and of course, the Bourbon Barrel Tour.

Legends

Tony Award-nominated actress Taylor Louderman hails from Bourbon. She is best known for originating the role of Regina George in Tina Fey's *Mean Girls* musical and for starring in *Bring It On: The Musical,* both on Broadway.

Vitals / Fun Facts

- Bourbon's water system was installed in the 1930s, with the water tower erected using horses. It is still functional today.
- The town's name was supposed to be St. Cloud, but the constant references to bourbon and the phrase "let's go to Bourbon!" led to the town being called "Bourbon in the Village of St. Cloud." This name was chosen when the post office was established, but eventually the name was shortened to simply "Bourbon."

Lore

The town was, in fact, named for the popular liquor. It is said that around the time the town was born, a local man opened a general store on his property to serve the needs of area settlers. There was a new liquor making the rounds called bourbon, and he ordered some barrels. People would gather at the store in the evenings to sample the liquor. A barrel with "bourbon" written on it sat on the porch of the store, and soon the barrel became a quick way to reference the store and the budding community. The name stuck.

Bourbon's original water tower just off of Highway 44 has become the symbol of the town.
Courtesy of Wikimedia Commons

BUTLER

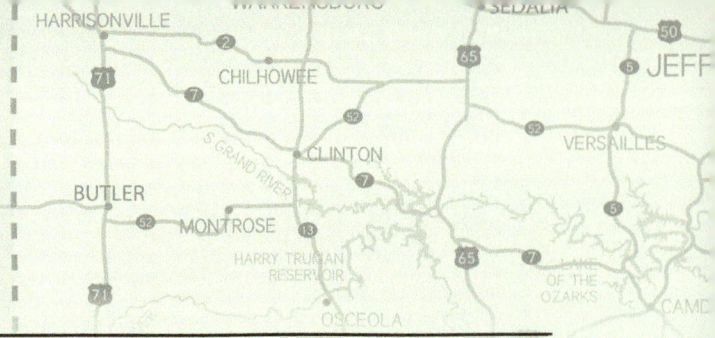

Bates County
POPULATION
4,220

Founding Story

Head west and follow the energy emanating from Butler, Missouri! Before the town of Butler was established, the first European settlers to the area were missionaries, who arrived to try to convert Native Americans to Christianity. The missionaries drew settlers, and after Native Americans were forcibly removed from Missouri, more permanent settlements were planted. Butler was officially platted in 1856, and its location and its early businesses made it a popular stop for those seeking their fortune during the Gold Rush years. During the Civil War, the Battle of Butler (also known as the Battle of Island Mound) was fought about eight miles southwest of Butler, and after the execution of Order #11, which forced the evacuation of four western Missouri counties, Butler had to be completely rebuilt. But, this rebuilding helped Butler propel the community into the future, modernizing their infrastructure and symbolizing progress in Missouri. Today, it remains a quaint small town and a hot spot for history lovers who long for the ambiance of the original brick streets, stately historic homes, and charming downtown square. It is also part of the Freedom's Frontier National Heritage Area, a 31,000-square-mile region in eastern Kansas and western Missouri that witnessed travelers along the Santa Fe, Oregon, California, and Mormon historic trails.

Butler's castle-like courthouse rises above the town square with its stone and clock tower.
Courtesy of Butler Main Street

Legends
If you've owned a computer with Windows XP, you've seen the operating system's default photo, called "Bliss." This iconic photo, seen by billions of people, was created by Butler native Charles O'Rear.

Lore
The Battle of Island Mound during the Civil War, also known as the Battle of Butler, included the first Kansas Colored Volunteer Infantry Regiment, the first Black infantry to fight in the Civil War.

Attractions
Check out the "Original Generator," explore the area's history at the Bates County Museum, walk the historic downtown, or learn more about the Civil War by visiting Battle of Island Mound State Historic Site.

Events
Butler hosts several annual events, such as its car show and Huckster's Day festival. Don't miss the Brick Street Bash with booths from local businesses and crafters.

Vitals / Fun Facts
- Butler is known as "The Electric City" because it was the first in Missouri to have electric power.
- Butler is often referred to as the city where the Civil War began in Missouri.

Memorial to Civil War Colored Troops
Courtesy of Bates County Museum

Butler was the first city to have electric power in the state, and you can still visit the original generator in town.
Courtesy of City of Butler

Butler's downtown represents a rich history and an important place in Missouri's story.
Courtesy of Butler Chamber of Commerce

CALEDONIA

Washington County — POPULATION **131**

Founding Story

Small but mighty Caledonia is a true rural Missouri destination. The town was founded in 1819, and the original plot of land was a portion of the Miles Goforth Spanish Land Grant. Located in the Ozark Foothills of Missouri, ownership of the land changed hands twice before the community was finally platted by Alexander Craighead. He bought the first lot and named the town Caledonia for his homeland of Scotland. Development of the community continued as more lots were purchased, schools and churches were built, and businesses were opened. Caledonia remained a small town and began to decline in the 20th century. By the early 2000s, Caledonia's downtown was struggling to retain businesses, and most buildings were empty. However, in recent years, a rise in small town tourism has inspired a renewed enthusiasm to bring life back to the downtown buildings and make the town a cultural heritage tourism must-see in Missouri. Now, downtown Caledonia is full of antique stores, quilt shops, eateries, and more to fill any visitor's itinerary.

The masonic lodge (left) is the oldest west of the Mississippi.
Courtesy of Legends of America

Caledonia's downtown draws in visitors with its bright colors, whimsical decor, and welcoming people.
Courtesy of Legends of America

Legends
Congressman Willard Vandiver is from Caledonia and is credited with inspiring our state's motto, "The Show Me State." He is quoted as saying, "I am from Missouri. You have to show me," during a speech at a banquet.

Lore
Fergus Sloan's Brewery was one of the first two businesses in town, but it was short-lived. The supposed reason, as Jacob Launius, pastor of the Methodist church from 1836 to 1837, wrote in his diary, was that "the brewery did not exist very long, because right in the beginning the Methodists were having a Camp Meeting and everyone got religion but one old drunken 'Sot.'" Thus, the brewery went out of business.

Grab a scoop and shop around at the Old Village Mercantile, in operation since 1909.
Courtesy of Old Village Mercantile

Attractions
In Caledonia, antiquing is a must. Visit the oldest Masonic lodge west of the Mississippi; treat yourself to ice cream at the Old Village Mercantile, which dates back to 1909; and stroll the Caledonia Historic District with more than 35 historic homes, buildings, and churches listed on the National Register of Historic Places.

Caledonia is the perfect town to visit if you love antique shops and unique small businesses.
Courtesy of Old Village Antiques

Events
Caledonia has many great events throughout the year, including its Vintage Market in May, Pumpkin Fest in October, and Christmas Market in December. It also has regular events throughout the year, like Music Pickin' in the Park, Just Junkin' market, and flea markets.

The Craighead-Henry House is the oldest property in Caledonia's historic district and was once home to Caledonia's founder, Alexander Craighead.
Courtesy of Missouri State Parks

Vitals / Fun Facts
- Caledonia is the smallest incorporated town in Missouri.
- Caledonia is Latin for "Scotland," which was founder Alexander Craighead's homeland.

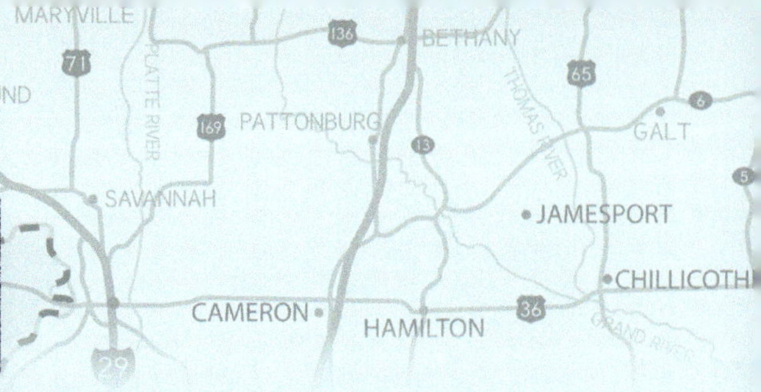

CAMERON

Clinton, DeKalb & Caldwell County
POPULATION 8,678

Founding Story

Cameron's story actually begins with the town of Somerville, which was established along the proposed route of the Hannibal-St. Joseph Railroad. Developers soon realized, however, that Somerville's grade was too steep for rail traffic, and they moved the town about a mile away to land that would be better suited for the railroad. Thus, a new community, called "The Crossroads of the Nation," was founded in 1855, and the town's name changed from Somerville to Cameron, after the founder's wife. The town did not have an official governing system for almost 10 years after its founding, but the community grew quickly as a center for agriculture, transportation, and commerce. The community has taken great strides to preserve both the town's stories and historic buildings, thanks to an active historical society and library with a bounty of resources. Cameron today is a prosperous Missouri community, with unique events and plenty of sites to experience during your visit.

Cameron calls itself the "Crossroads of the Nation" because of its location in mid-Missouri and its role as an important railroad depot.
Courtesy of the City of Cameron

McCorkle Park is a lovely community gathering space that hosts free performances by the Cameron Municipal Band.
Courtesy of the City of Cameron

Legends
Stage and film actor DeWitt Clarke Jennings was born in Cameron. Between 1906 and 1920, he acted in over a dozen Broadway plays, and in more than 150 films between 1915 and 1937.

Lore
Cameron was chosen as the filming location for the 1969 film *Adam at 6 A.M.*, starring Michael Douglas. Many recognizable town spots and locals as extras can be seen in the film.

Attractions
Cameron is a town for history lovers. Visit the Depot Museum, the Old School, and the Musser Mansion. Honor those who served at the Veterans Memorial, and take a historic walking tour or cemetery tour.

Events
Cameron is known for its free concerts in McCorkle Park, which take place Memorial Day through August.

Vitals / Fun Facts
- William Jennings Bryan, two-time presidential candidate, delivered a passionate, heated speech in McCorkle Park in 1901.
- The town's original location was not suited for the incoming Hannibal-St. Joseph railroad, so to ensure its spot on the railroad, the town hooked up teams of oxen to the three buildings in town (then known as Somerville) and moved them about a mile or so southwest.
- The Cameron Municipal Band dates to 1866, and voters decided in 1929 to pass a tax to ensure the band remains supported. To this day, the band is one of only a few tax-supported city bands in the country.

DeWitt Clarke Jennings
Courtesy of Wikimedia Commons

There are many examples of beautifully preserved and restored historic homes in Cameron. Pictured here is the Sanders Mansion.
Courtesy of My Cameron News

The restored depot in Cameron represents the town's history as a railroad community, which helped it grow and prosper in its early years.
Courtesy of Cameron Depot Museum

CARL JUNCTION

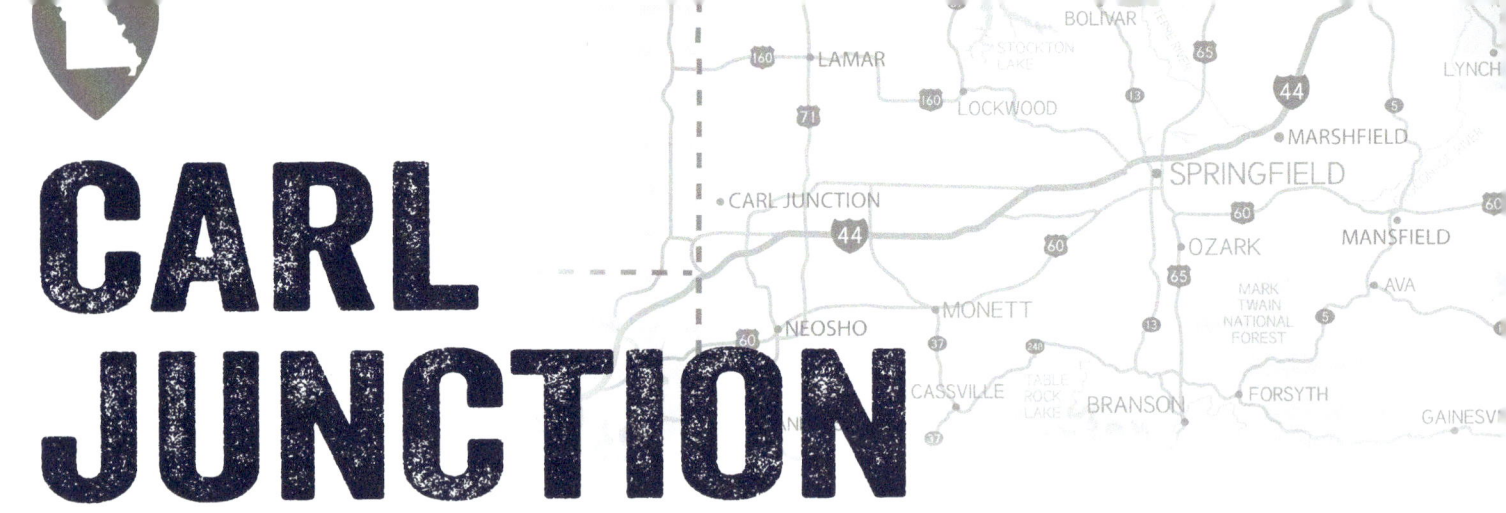

Jasper County
POPULATION
8,366

Founding Story

The name "Carl Junction" refers to both the town's founder and its place in railroad history as the junction of two railroads. In its early days, Carl Junction's main attraction for settlers was lead mining, and as the mining industry grew, the town was added to the railroad line. Trains began traveling through Carl Junction in 1879 and the town grew up around a railroad economy, and within a decade added a railroad section facility, switching yard, coal and water chute, a depot, and an office. The railroad and related facilities were major employers during the town's beginnings, and banks, boarding houses, hotels, and apartments were soon added to the town as well—with the boarding houses and apartments consistently at 100 percent capacity in the early 20th century. The community today is one beaming with pride and eager to show visitors what small-town hospitality is all about.

Carl Junction is named for its location at the junction of two railroads, and today it is a quiet, peaceful community in the scenic Ozarks.

Legends
Though not a person, the tornado is a legend in Carl Junction to be sure. The community has seen its fair share of destructive tornadoes over the generations, most recently in 2019 and 2024. However, the town is resilient and has shown that nothing, not even a mighty tornado, can keep this town down.

Lore
In 1892, the eyes of the world were on Carl Junction when a nearby mine unearthed the fossilized remains of two adult and two juvenile *Elephas americanus*—an extinct species of elephant. Thought to be the largest ever found at that time, the remains were displayed at the World's Columbian Exposition, aka the Chicago World's Fair, in 1893.

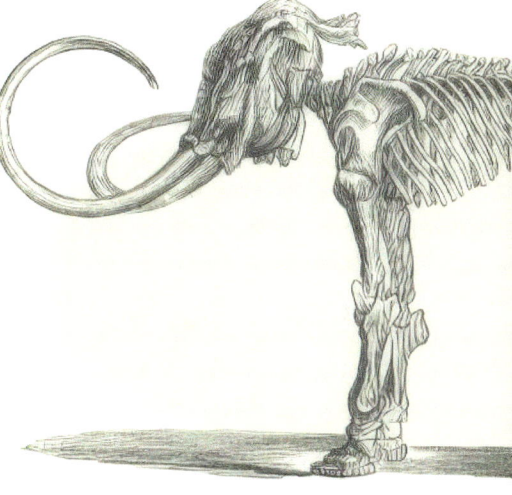
A fascinating piece of Carl Junction's history is the fossilized remains of an early species of elephant, two adults and two juveniles. Found in 1892, the remains were displayed at the Chicago World's Fair the following year.
Courtesy of Carl Junction Historic Preservation Committee

Attractions
The great outdoors await in Carl Junction. Visit beautiful Center Creek Park; play a round or two at scenic Briarbrook Golf Course; or enjoy Bulldog Lake, Carl Junction Access, and Thom Station Trail.

Events
For great music, visit the annual Bluegrass Festival. You can also peruse booths of local food and goods at Second Tuesday in the Park or bring the family to the Crafts Fall Festival.

Center Creek Park is a popular spot for outdoor recreation.

Vitals / Fun Facts
- Carl Junction is one dedicated community. Its library, community center, and inclusive playground are just three examples of entities that were built purely from community fundraising.

Carl Junction is proud to have a large inclusive playground on its school grounds, built through fundraising.
Courtesy of Missouri Humanities

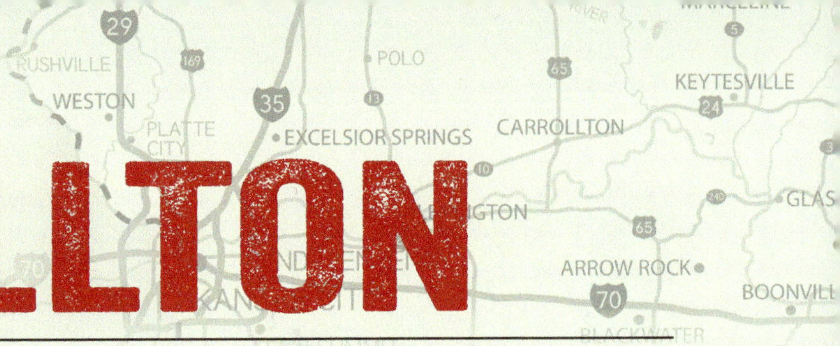

CARROLLTON

Carroll County
POPULATION
3,637

Founding Story

The first family of settlers of what would become Carrollton came in the late 1820s. The town was established at the junction of the Grand and Missouri Rivers, and officially founded in 1833. When Carroll County was being planned, the original name was intended to be Wakenda, named for a small river that went through the county. However, upon Charles Carroll's (of Carrollton) death in 1832, the name was decided as Carroll County, to honor Carroll's contribution to our nation's history as the last surviving signer of the Declaration of Independence. The first family, the Wilcoxson family, opened a general store, ran a successful real estate business, and started a banking firm that remained in the family until the 1930s. The railroad was responsible for much of Carrollton's growth, like many northern Missouri towns. Industry grew in Carroll County to support railroad commerce, and large-scale farming was soon growing as well. Today, agriculture remains a major industry in the area, but it is also home to unique shops, beautiful outdoor amenities, a thriving downtown, and many historic sites.

If small-town charm and hospitality are on your wish list, Carrollton is the place to be!
Courtesy of My Hometown Carrollton

Legends
Brigadier General James Shields is from Carrollton. He was a Civil War general and a US senator from three different states, and he almost dueled Abraham Lincoln. Shields moved here after the Civil War and remained until his death in 1879.

Lore
Carroll County's roots run deep. Long before this area was part of Missouri, the first known European settlement in what eventually became Carroll County was at Fort Orleans in the 1720s. However, the fort lasted only a few years, and so far, no physical evidence has been found of the site. The Daughters of the American Revolution erected a historic marker at Wiese Roadside Park that recounts this brief but interesting history.

Visiting Carrollton during the holiday season feels like walking onto the set of a Hallmark movie.
Courtesy of My Hometown Carrollton

Attractions
Carrollton and the surrounding area have beautiful outdoor amenities such as Cranberry Bend National Fish and Wildlife Refuge, Grand Pass Conservation Area, and Van Meter State Park. Take a stroll through the streets around downtown Carrollton to appreciate the historic homes, and be sure to check out La Bella Casa. To learn more about the area, visit the Carroll County Museum. And be sure to shop at the Carroll County Mercantile and grab a bite at the Burger Bar and Dari Maid (going on 75+ years!).

Events
Carrollton keeps the community energized with its First Friday events in the spring and summer, the Carroll County Fair, Halloween parades, trolley ride tours, Sippin' on the Square, holiday markets, Lighted Christmas Parade, and Holiday Homes Tour.

Vitals / Fun Facts
- Carrollton won the 2005 All-America City Award from the National Civic League, which recognizes communities that successfully address local issues in innovative ways using civic engagement, collaboration, and inclusivity.
- In 1804, Lewis and Clark stopped in what eventually became Carroll County as they went upriver, and they carved oars out of the plentiful timber in the floodplain.

La Bella Casa was built in 1912 but has been newly restored as an event center with lodging in the manor.
Courtesy of La Bella Casa

CHILLICOTHE

Livingston County
POPULATION
9,107

Founding Story

Visitors to Chillicothe will marvel at the town's charm, historic sites, and exciting events. Chillicothe was founded in 1834, named after a town in Ohio of the same name, which is derived from a Shawnee word meaning "big town" or "big town where we live." Chillicothe, Missouri, became a vital railroad community in the 1850s along the Hannibal-St. Joseph Railroad, and the town also developed a thriving agriculture industry. Chillicothe has grown and made a name for itself as an important community along the Highway 36 corridor in northern Missouri, especially since rediscovering the town's ties to a monumental innovation—sliced bread. The town has woven its story into many facets of the community, celebrating the fascinating people, connections, and innovations that have come from this energetic and progressive Missouri town.

Visitors to Chillicothe can fill their day exploring the arts district, finding souvenirs at fun shops, learning about local history, and enjoying delicious food.
Courtesy of Visit Chillicothe

Legends

Otto Rohwedder is the man, the myth, the legend who brought sliced bread to the public, inventing a machine to slice loaves of bread into uniform pieces, selling the first loaves of pre-sliced bread right here in Chillicothe.

Lore

What if Rohwedder hadn't succeeded? It was a possibility! As he was working on his invention, he became ill. Doctors thought he had little time to live and urged him to forget the invention and focus on getting his affairs in order. Rohwedder ignored the doctors and went on to live long enough for his machine to make it to bakeries.

Attractions

Visit the Home of Sliced Bread as you begin your adventure in Chillicothe, where you'll learn more about Chillicothe's history and receive guidance on what's going on in town. To learn more about the area's story, check out the Grand River Historical Society Museum. You can't miss the murals throughout the downtown area, and be sure to stroll the arts district. If you're looking for a unique place for a souvenir, shop at the Salty Hippo Studio for hand-printed goods and other local finds.

Events

You can enjoy the annual Chautauqua in the Park Festival, and the Sliced Bread Day Festival each year is a must-see.

Vitals / Fun Facts

- The Grand River Historical Society Museum has on display one of the earliest models of Otto Rohwedder's bread-slicing machine—on loan from the Smithsonian!
- In keeping with the town's roots as the home of sliced bread, local café Boji Stone serves bread pudding a little differently—cut into slices!

Ever heard the saying "greatest thing since sliced bread"? Well, Chillicothe takes that personally as the birthplace of this incredible innovation!

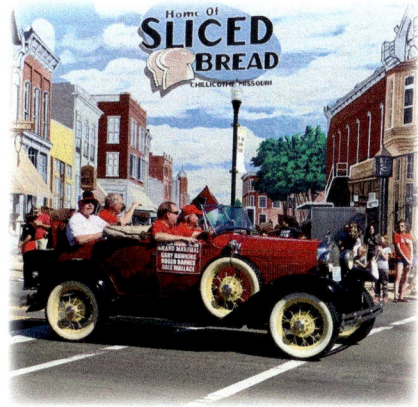

Every year, Chillicothe celebrates during its Sliced Bread Day Festival.
Courtesy of Visit Chillicothe

Chillicothe Aerial
Courtesy of Missouri Humanities

Visit Cuba to see the World's Largest Rocker (so says the *Guinness Book of World Records*)!
Courtesy of Angie Barrett

CUBA

Founding Story

Visitors looking for a place where art, nature, and history connect should look no further than Cuba. Prior to the community's founding in 1857, this region was home to ancestral lands of the Osage Nation, and the area witnessed the tragic events of Indian Removal along the Trail of Tears. The first non-native settler was William Harrison in 1821, but additional settlers were slow to come at first. The population eventually started to grow more steadily when the town of Cuba was formally established to support the anticipated southern branch of the Union Pacific Railroad, with St. Louis being a frequent customer of goods produced by the lucrative farming and mining industries in and around Cuba.

Iron mining began in Cuba in 1869 and was a main contributor to the early growth and development of the town at the time, continuing to be a major employer and industry for over 50 years.

Crawford County — Population 3,181

A town directory published in 1881 notes over 60 businesses in Cuba, helping to serve the needs of the growing community. That growth continued into the 20th century as Route 66 was completed through Cuba in 1931, a catalyst for economic growth as new businesses emerged and restaurants, motels, filling and service stations, and more sprouted up along the highway to fill the needs of increased traffic. Today, over a dozen of these Route 66 sites still exist and can be seen throughout the area as visitors traverse the historic highway.

In the town of Cuba, history isn't just kept within the confines of a museum, historical society, or library; it's on display for all to see throughout the community. A stunning array of over a dozen painted murals all over the town tell the story of Cuba in a striking and creative way. In fact, the town was named the Route 66 Mural City by the Missouri House and Senate to commemorate Cuba's commitment to sharing history through artistic storytelling, which has helped Cuba grow as a tourist attraction.

Courtesy of Guy Randall

Cuba honors the Osage Nation and their connection to the land on which the town sits with a monument right off the highway exit.
Courtesy of Phelps County Focus

 Legends

The town of Cuba holds the Osage Nation in high regard, as the community recognizes the ancestral and cultural connection of the Osage to this land. The location of Cuba was an integral part of the Osage Trail, used for travel and trade between the area and St. Louis. Cuba honors the Osage with the Osage Legacy Monument, located at exit 208 on Highway 44 in Cuba, which depicts an Osage warrior and his family in period dress heading westward.

 Lore

George Jamison, an early store owner in what was to become Cuba, wanted to name the new town Amanda after his wife. However, sympathy for the island of Cuba was common among his customers as Cuba fought for its independence from Spain. According to legend, Jamison's customers cast lots to choose the town name, and Cuba was the winner.

Two examples of Route 66 buildings include the Weir on 66 restaurant and Shelly's Route 66 Cafe.
Courtesy of Weir on 66

Attractions

The Cuba Mural Trail is a must see, along with the many Route 66-era buildings, such as the Wagon Wheel Motel. Traverse the Antique Trail to find that special something, and for a bit of area history, head to the Crawford County Historical Society Museum. And of course, it's impossible to miss the Osage Trail Legacy Monument, a powerful reminder of those who were here before us.

Events

The town is best known for its annual Cuba Fest and for hosting the Crawford County Fair.

Vitals / Fun Facts

- Cuba is a proud Route 66 Mural City, with 15+ murals throughout the community beautifully combining art and history to tell Cuba's story.
- At Hayes Family Shoe Store, you can view a cardboard cutout of the tallest man to ever live and see his size 37 shoes!

The Historic Wagon Wheel Motel
Courtesy of Wagon Wheel Motel

Cuba is called the Route 66 Mural City.
Courtesy of Viva Cuba, Inc.

Cuba is a popular stop along historic Route 66 because of its well-preserved buildings and businesses.
Courtesy of Visit Cuba, Inc.

DEFIANCE

St. Charles County
POPULATION 159

Founding Story

Like many other towns in this region, the town of Defiance was formed because of the coming of the Katy railroad, and with that eventually came a depot and post office. Prior to this, the area was explored by Daniel Boone and his cohort, who were the sole settlers west of the river by the start of the 19th century. The town's name is said to come from the fact that the neighboring town of Matson doubted that this burgeoning town would be able to obtain a depot, a post office, and all else that comes with it, but in fact, Defiance succeeded. Today, Defiance is a popular place to rest and recharge along the Katy Trail and scenic Highway 94. Visitors will enjoy the casual, charming restaurants and bars, serene setting, and slower pace that Defiance offers.

Legends

Legendary frontiersman Daniel Boone and his family lived on a homestead in Defiance in the early 19th century. The Boone family had quite the legacy, with Daniel and his wife having 11 children, who went on to give them 70 grandchildren and more than 250 great-grandchildren.

Daniel Boone
Courtesy of the State Historical Society of Missouri

Defiance is considered the gateway to Missouri Wine Country, and the town is full of activity during the late spring, summer, and early fall when tourists flock to the area.
Courtesy of Defiance Ridge Vineyard

Daniel Boone Home
Courtesy of St. Charles County Parks

Lore

Daniel Boone and his family have many stories attached to their name and their time in Defiance—maybe true, maybe not! One popular tale is that Boone had a rifle named "Tick-Licker" because his shot was so precise, he could hit a tick off an animal without hurting the beast. No one seemed to argue this one!

Attractions

In Defiance, the beautiful wineries are a must-visit—a perfect way to unwind from a day on the Katy Trail or hiking in nearby Weldon Spring or August A. Busch Memorial Conservation Areas. While in the area, learn about some fascinating local history at the Weldon Spring Site Interpretive Center and climb to the top of the gravel containment cell for the best view of the area. If you're in need of more outdoor options, head to Klondike Park or Broemmelsiek Park (with an educational garden and astronomy viewing area), and be sure to tour the Historic Daniel Boone Home.

If you're up for a challenge, climb the stairs of the Weldon Spring Site's containment cell for the best view of the area.
Courtesy of the Municipal Magazine

Events

For fun times in Defiance, check out its annual St Patrick's Day Festival and Christmas Festival, live music at the wineries, weekly stargazing programs at Broemmelsiek Park, and living history programs at the Daniel Boone Home.

Vitals / Fun Facts

- State Highway 94 through Defiance is often called the Missouri Weinstrasse ("Wine Street") because of the numerous vineyards in the area, and Defiance is known as the Gateway to Missouri Wine Country.

Defiance may seem small, but there are multiple restaurants, breweries, wineries, and shops to cater to busy tourists and community members.
Courtesy of Discover St. Charles

The Heritage Homestead provides visitors with an immersive experience with historic buildings. It's also where you'll find the blacksmiths at work on Saturday mornings!

DONIPHAN

Founding Story

Doniphan is a beautiful Ozark community renowned for its great outdoor amenities, festivals, and historic sites. Founded in 1847, the area was settled because of its ideal location within the Ozarks and along the Current River. For a time, plans were made to extend the St. Louis, Iron Mountain, and Southern Railroad to Doniphan from Pilot Knob, but the coming and eventual constant conflict of the Civil War halted plans. Doniphan saw heavy fighting during the Civil War because of its strategic location, and guerilla warfare was rampant in the area. As Sterling Price advanced on southeastern Missouri, Union troops burned Doniphan.

Though the town was devastated during and after the war, regrowth came soon with the building of the railroad through Doniphan. The arrival of the Missouri Pacific Railroad in the 1880s brought the promise of economic prosperity, particularly as a booming railroad tie and logging industry began thanks to all the native pine in the area. Trees were cut and floated down the Current River to Doniphan, where they were milled and shipped off. Doniphan and surrounding Ripley County quickly became a leader in railroad tie production, and at its peak, the Missouri Tie and Lumber Company cut and shipped up to 35 million feet of logs annually.

As the logging industry cleared much of the land of trees, farmers began to move in and establish a thriving agricultural industry. The logging industry dominated the area for many decades until the Great Depression, but agriculture remained a necessary occupation. New businesses and manufacturing during and after World War II helped Doniphan bounce back, and tourism began to increase as Doniphan became a destination in Missouri for outdoor and river recreation. Today, the area is working to restore its forests after the effects of the logging industry, and the area continues to offer unparalleled outdoor experiences. Doniphan attracts thousands of visitors each year to float the crystal clear Current River, camp and explore Mark Twain National Forest, and take a step back in time during community heritage events.

Ripley County
POPULATION
1,781

Billy Yates
Courtesy of Wikimedia Commons

Legends

Award-winning country singer and songwriter Billy Yates was born and raised in Doniphan, and he still owns a home in the area. Bob Lewis, bluegrass phenom and founder of the Bob Lewis Family Band, owned a music store in Doniphan until his death in 2023.

Lore

Is Doniphan haunted? Several places in town have been the subject of spooky happenings, like figures appearing in the courthouse windows, apparitions in the old hospital, and mysterious voices in a certain shop on the square.

Doniphan's downtown boasts a historic courthouse at the center surrounded by museums, historic sites, restaurants, and shops.
Courtesy of Discover Doniphan Missouri

Attractions

While in Doniphan, learn about the area's history at the Current River Heritage Museum and visit the historic structures at the Heritage Homestead. If the river calls to you, head to Rocky River Resort to camp and float the pristine Current River. The town also has a well-known quilting store with unique fabrics and patterns.

Events

Visit the farmers' market, celebrate Heritage Days, kick back with some music at Pickin' on the Square, or enjoy crafting at the Annual Quilt Show.

Vitals / Fun Facts

- The Heritage Homestead is the only place in the state other than Silver Dollar City in Branson that offers traditional blacksmithing demonstrations on a regular basis.
- Visit the Current River Heritage Museum for an impressive collection of locally made gigs (and for some . . . come to learn what a gig is!).

The Current River is the number one destination in town for floating, boating, and fishing.
Courtesy of Rocky River Resort

Doniphan is proud to share and celebrate its history during its annual Heritage Days festival.
Courtesy of Discover Doniphan Missouri

Doniphan is the only place in the state other than Silver Dollar City to offer regular blacksmithing demos that are open to the public.

EMINENCE

Shannon County • POPULATION 515

Founding Story

The history of this picturesque Ozarks community is a tale of two cities! The Eminence we know today was established in 1868, but it was not the first. Interest in the area by white settlers began as early as the 1830s when Missouri's first copper mine opened, followed by timber harvesting from the dense forests in the second half of the 19th century. During the Civil War, the original town was badly damaged as both Union and Confederate troops raided mercilessly through the Ozark region, and many buildings in "Old Eminence" were burned. When rebuilding, town leaders took advantage of this opportunity to build the "new Eminence" in a location that would better suit the needs of the growing community. Eminence was rebuilt on the Jacks Fork River, which was seen as more accessible than its previous location, and made the county seat of Shannon County. Stories differ as to why the location was chosen, but if you ask the tourists, they'll say they're glad it was picked! Eminence has grown into a sought-after town for its renowned Ozark beauty, river and other outdoor recreation, and fascinating history.

Legends

Mitch Jayne, author and musician from the Dillards, was from Eminence. The Dillards helped popularize bluegrass music and appeared on the *Andy Griffith Show* as the Darling family.

Float the beautiful Jacks Fork River during your trip to Eminence and see why people call this river one of the most scenic in the state!
Courtesy of Visit Eminence

Mitch Jayne
Courtesy of Missouri Folk Arts

40 | SMALL TOWN MISSOURI

Lore
The original town, "Old Eminence," was actually established about 12 miles away from present-day Eminence. The town was moved in favor of a more accessible, central location for the county seat. Later, archaeologists excavated the area and confirmed where a courthouse and jail would have been, but no other structures. They did find 19th-century artifacts and the lock plate for the jail.

Attractions
Natural beauty awaits in Eminence. Visit Echo Bluff State Park, float or camp on the Jacks Fork River, explore the surrounding Ozark National Scenic Riverways, and take in the history (and snap some amazing pictures!) at Alley Mill in Alley Spring State Park.

Eminence was once located about 12 miles from its current location, but it was destroyed during the Civil War.
Courtesy of Missouri Independent

Events
The annual Ozark Mountain Festival is the perfect event to experience Eminence's Ozark culture and beauty.

Vitals/Fun Facts
- The original town was burned during the prevalent guerilla warfare during the Civil War, and Eminence was rebuilt in 1868 in a different location on the Jacks Fork of the Current River.
- Eminence is part of the Ozark National Scenic Riverways, which serves as Missouri's largest national park and the nation's first protected river system.
- Eminence is one of the few places in the Midwest where you can still see wild horses.

Possibly one of the most photographed spots in rural Missouri is Alley Mill.
Courtesy of National Park Service

Eminence is one of the last places visitors can still see wild horses.
Courtesy of Visit Eminence

EXCELSIOR SPRINGS

Founding Story

If you're looking for a step back in time, look no further than Excelsior Springs. Founded in 1880, the area that would become the town of Excelsior Springs gained popularity as people heard of the healing qualities of the area's mineral springs. Siloam Spring, whose water was a reddish color, was the first spring discovered by settlers in the area and is the spring credited with jump-starting the growth of Excelsior Springs. With 20 separate springs— including rare iron-manganese springs— producing four different kinds of mineral water, the town easily marketed itself as a destination for those who believed in the healing properties of the springs.

Word spread, hotels and spas were built, and Excelsior Springs remained a major tourist attraction for decades. In addition to the spa experience, the waters from the springs were often bottled and sold, as well as used to make other kinds of beverages like sodas. In fact, water from the Soterian well was used to make the award-winning Soterian Ginger Ale, which received medals at both the Chicago World's Fair in 1893 and the St. Louis World's Fair in 1904. The community continued steady growth during the first part of the 20th century, and luxury hotels like the Elms were sought after by Missouri's elite.

Construction of Excelsior Springs's grand centerpiece—the Hall of Waters— was completed in 1938. Constructed in stunning Art Deco style and decorated with water symbols and nods to water gods, the plumbing system in the Hall of Waters pumped water from 10 different springs into the world's longest mineral bar, which visitors can still see today. Though the popularity of mineral spas dwindled into the latter part of the 20th century, visitors can still stay in the beautiful Elms Hotel, which was a luxurious destination in the town's heyday. Most of the springs that propelled Excelsior Springs's growth are no longer visible, but efforts are being made to restore some of the spots marking the springs, and the town has kept interest alive with a lively downtown, unique shops and restaurants, and must-visit historic sites.

The Elms Hotel is a historic property in Excelsior Springs that remains an active hotel, spa, and event center.

Brenda Joyce
Courtesy of Wikimedia Commons

Legends
Actress Brenda Joyce, who portrayed Jane in the 1940s Tarzan films, is from Excelsior Springs.

Lore
There are many stories of the healing properties of the water at Siloam Spring. One in particular is the story of a local farmer, Mr. Mellion, who was looking for treatment for his daughter's tuberculosis. He was persuaded to have her try the water at the spring to drink and bathe in, and she saw significant improvement in just a few days, and was cured within weeks. Another story tells of a Civil War veteran who decided to test the healing properties by soaking a gunshot wound to his leg that hadn't healed, and miraculously, another tale for the books was born as the wound began to heal.

Attractions
For the full Excelsior Springs experience, book a stay and spa treatments at the historic Elms Hotel. Visit the Hall of Waters to step back in time to Excelsior Springs's heyday as a spring water destination, and be sure to stop into Willow Springs Mercantile for local goods as you traverse the picturesque downtown.

This historic postcard offers a glance at Excelsior Springs during its height as a major tourist attraction and a spa and resort community.
Courtesy of Main Street America

Events
Excelsior Springs hosts an annual Waterfest, wine festival, and BBQ and Fly-in on the River.

Vitals/Fun Facts
- President Harry S. Truman spent his election night at the Elms Hotel.
- Siloam Spring was the first of the mineral waters discovered in Excelsior Springs. It is the only natural supply of ferro-manganese mineral water in the United States and one of only five known worldwide.

The Hall of Waters went through extensive restoration and now stands as a symbol of the town and its history.

FULTON

Callaway County
POPULATION 12,600

Founding Story

Founded in 1825 and serving as the seat of Callaway County, Fulton is a thriving small town first settled by folks migrating along the Missouri River and Boone's Lick Trail. The town has deep agricultural roots and played an important role in the railroad industry in the late 19th century. Its location near the Missouri River, the railroad, and major thoroughfares made it an ideal location for businesses and farms. The community is steeped in history, from its in-demand brick manufacturing, its role as an educational center in the state, and even its international fame gained by a visit from Sir Winston Churchill. Today, Fulton boasts beautiful historic homes, a thriving downtown, and great annual events for visitors to experience as they immerse themselves in this energetic small town.

Legends

Nick Cave, internationally renowned sculptor, dancer, and performance artist, is from Fulton. He's known for his "Soundsuits" that blend fashion and sculpture. He's created art in subway stations in New York City and has had work exhibited at the Museum of Contemporary Art Chicago; the Solomon R. Guggenheim Museum in New York; the Smithsonian American Art Museum in Washington, DC; and the Museum of Modern Art in New York.

Courtesy of Kingdom of Callaway Historical Society

While in Fulton, grab a slice (or a whole pie!) at Brooklyn Pizza for the best New York–style pizza outside New York.
Courtesy of Notley Hawkins

Lore
It might be hard to imagine for little ol' Missouri, but the one and only Sir Winston Churchill, prime minister of the United Kingdom, delivered one of his most famous speeches at Westminster College in Fulton. This particular speech condemned Soviet Union policies and was the first time the term "Iron Curtain" was used to describe the division of the European continent: "From Stettin in the Baltic to Trieste in the Adriatic, an iron curtain has descended across the continent."

Attractions
Because of Fulton's role in its history, you can view a large piece of the Berlin Wall on the campus of Westminster College. You can learn more about it at America's National Churchill Museum. Stroll the historic Brick District, view the beautifully restored and maintained historic homes on Court Street, and tour the scenic campuses of Fulton's two colleges.

Events
Come to Fulton for Third Thursday in the Brick District, dirt track races, the Rough Riders Horse Show, and the annual Fulton Street Fair.

Vitals / Fun Facts
- Fulton is the home of the Missouri School for the Deaf, the first such school west of the Mississippi.
- Fulton State Hospital is one of the first three mental health institutions west of the Mississippi.

Fulton's connection to Winston Churchill enabled the community to obtain a large piece of the Berlin Wall that is on display on Westminster College's campus.
Courtesy of America's National Churchill Museum

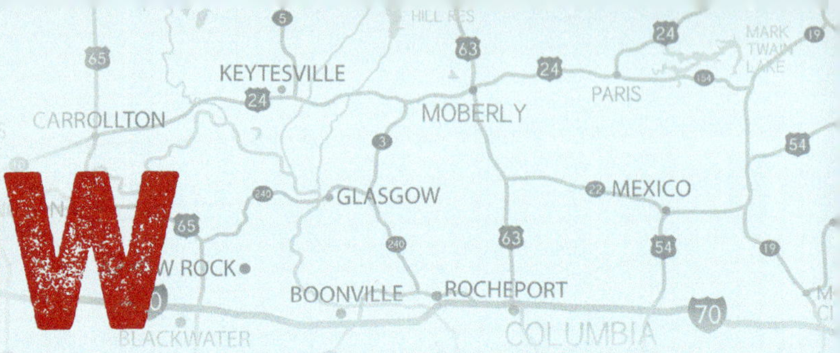

GLASGOW

Howard County
POPULATION
1,087

Founding Story

Founded in 1836, Glasgow was technically founded by 13 men, though the town was named for just one of them: James Glasgow, who was from St. Louis. The town grew quickly thanks to the successful agricultural economy of growing hemp and tobacco. Soon, several local businesses, churches, banks, and saloons occupied the downtown and helped provide many of the necessary services for a budding community. As automobiles edged out the railroad and other communities put toll bridges in place, Glasgow opened a free bridge, a nod to the town's commitment to infrastructure and accessibility. The town takes pride in its rich history, evident by the historic photos and newspaper clippings that adorn local establishments and the community's efforts to restore and maintain sites imperative to telling Glasgow's story. The community is warm and welcoming, and is eager to share its special places and stories with visitors near and far.

Small-town charm radiates from Glasgow's main street district.
Courtesy of Glasgow Main Street

Legends

Carr Waller Pritchett, an astronomer and professor, is from Glasgow. He is best known as the first president of the Pritchett School Institute (later Pritchett College) in Glasgow and the first director of the Morrison Observatory, which is now in Fayette, Missouri.

Lore

A story from Glasgow's past that connects to a Glasgow institution is the story of Dr. Osborne Henderson. As an apprentice doctor, Henderson was witness to a gnarly amputation in the wilderness and was made to carry the amputated limb to town. The event took a toll on Henderson, who switched careers and opened a pharmacy instead in 1841. Henderson's Drug Store has been a staple in the community ever since.

Reserve a campsite at Stump Island Conservation Area for river recreation and breathtaking sunsets.
Courtesy of Missouri Conservation

Attractions

While in town, visit the Glasgow Museum, Henderson's Drug Store, and Rolling Pin Bakery; take a Historic Glasgow Scenic Driving Tour; see Stump Island; and visit the oldest continuously operating public library west of the Mississippi—the Lewis Library.

Henderson's Drug Store opened in Glasgow in 1841 and continues to operate under the same family, now in its sixth generation.
Courtesy of Columbia Missourian

Events

There are lots of great events throughout the year in Glasgow. Some favorites include its Wine Walk, annual Piccadilly, Missouri River Muscle Car Show, Jammin' on the River, Holiday in the Park, and Glasgow Kids Market.

Glasgow Lewis Library is the oldest continuously operating public library west of the Mississippi River.
Courtesy of Missouri Marker Database

The Chicago & Alton Bridge that crosses into Glasgow over the Missouri River was the first bridge in the world constructed completely from steel.
Courtesy of Downtown Different

Vitals / Fun Facts

- Henderson's Drug Store is the oldest single-family-operated drugstore west of the Mississippi. It opened in 1841 and is now in its sixth generation.
- Glasgow's Chicago & Alton Bridge, built in 1879, was the first bridge in the world constructed completely from steel.
- Glasgow is home to the sharpest bend on the Missouri River.

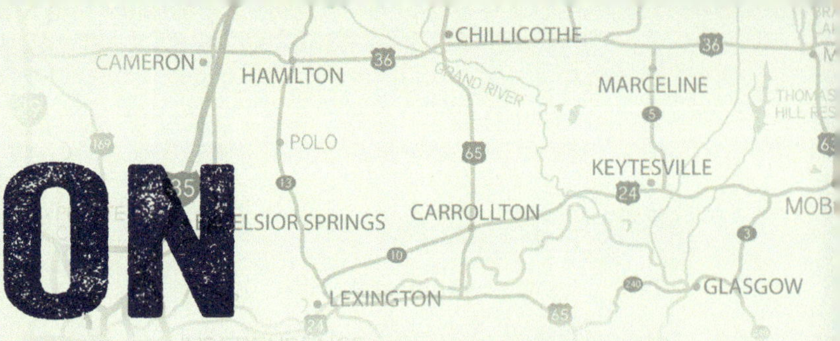

HAMILTON

Caldwell County
POPULATION
1,690

Founding Story

Another bustling Highway 36 community not to be missed is Hamilton, whose story helps defend the highway's nickname as "The Way of American Genius." Before Hamilton was founded in 1859, the area was prairie land belonging to the US government. The town was established to help support the building of the Hannibal-St. Joseph Railroad, and the first train to arrive in town came the same day the railroad was completed. Hamilton is reportedly named for two Hamiltons: founding father Alexander Hamilton and Joseph Hamilton, who died during the War of 1812. This Missouri community prospered like many railroad towns at the time, with businesses and residences sprouting up as a result. However, unlike Missouri railroad towns, Hamilton didn't experience as much turmoil as others during the Civil War. Though the town experienced some decline during the latter half of the 20th century, interest in the community grew once more with the opening of Missouri Star Quilt Company. Hamilton has since become a destination for quilting lovers young and old and has been called the "Disneyland of Quilting" because of the Missouri Quilt Museum and the town's 12 quilt shops.

The Penney's Quilt Shop storefront was J. C. Penney's original store.
Courtesy of Historical Marker Database

Legends
Hamilton is the birthplace of American businessman and department store icon James Cash (J. C.) Penney.

James Cash (J. C.) Penney
Courtesy of Highway 36 Heritage Alliance

Lore
After his retail business took off, J. C. Penney remained close to Hamilton and donated funds to build the first library, the shoe factory, the high school, Highland Cemetery, and the American Legion Park.

Attractions
You can't miss Missouri Star Quilt Company or the Missouri Quilt Museum, but be sure to check out the J. C. Penney Museum, see the World's Tallest Spool of Thread, and find out why Hamilton is part of the Highway 36 "Way of American Genius."

The Missouri Star Quilt Company helped make Hamilton a quilting destination.
Courtesy of Missouri Star Quilt Company

Events
Visit for the annual J. C. Penney Days; see the holiday tree-lighting; or attend quilting retreats, classes, and demos.

Vitals / Fun Facts
- In 2008, Missouri Star Quilt Company opened in Hamilton. From one long-arm quilting machine and two bolts of fabric, MSQC has grown to become the largest vendor of pre-cut fabric in the world, and the town is home to 12 quilt shops.

The J. C. Penney Memorial Library and Museum preserves the story of Hamilton and its history of innovation.
Courtesy of Missouri Star Quilt Company

For a touch of whimsy, visit the World's Largest Spool of Thread.
Courtesy of Missouri Star Quilt Company

SMALL TOWN MISSOURI | 51

HANNIBAL

Marion/Ralls Counties
POPULATION 17,108

Founding Story

Hannibal is home to legendary figures, fascinating lore, and entertainment for all ages. Hannibal is known around the world for being the boyhood home of Samuel Clemens (aka Mark Twain!), but come for a visit and discover how much more this lovely river community can show you. Founded in 1819, Hannibal is a river town that grew quickly as a port city for steamboats, flatboats, and more. The completion of the Hannibal-St. Joseph railroad in 1859 propelled the town forward, and the population and industry in town flourished with this new method of transportation and commerce. The town grew steadily into a tourist attraction in the 20th century as the community began sharing the stories of Mark Twain and his writings' connections to Hannibal, and today there are many events, sites, shops, and activities to make for a full visit.

A statue of Huck Finn and Tom Sawyer honors the stories that have made Hannibal famous.
Courtesy of Hamilton CVB

Samuel Clemens's boyhood home in Hannibal
Courtesy of the Library of Congress

Legends

You want legendary locals? Hannibal has 'em! Maybe you've heard of Samuel Clemens, better known by his pen name, Mark Twain. Or perhaps the "Unsinkable" Molly Brown, who survived the sinking of the *Titanic*, portrayed by Kathy Bates in the blockbuster film and inspiring a musical about her story? Or maybe you're more of a Disney fan and have heard the likes of Jiminy Cricket, voiced by Cliff Edwards? Well, all of these legends come from Hannibal.

Mark Twain
Courtesy of the Library of Congress

Molly Brown
Courtesy of Britannica

Lore

A well-known tale in the area is the story of Lovers Leap. A daughter of the Fox tribe and an Illini brave were deeply in love and, after multiple warnings to stop seeing each other, they were discovered together by the Fox chief one night on the cliff that is now called Lovers Leap. The couple leaped from the cliff together but survived the jump.

Attractions

Some must-see spots in Hannibal include the Mark Twain Boyhood Home and Museum, Jim's Journey: The Huck Finn Freedom Center, Mark Twain Cave, the Molly Brown House, the Becky Thatcher House, the Hannibal History Museum, and the Wax Museum. Hannibal is also part of the 50 Miles of Art corridor, and you won't want to miss Millionaire's Row or the Rockcliffe Mansion in the Maple Avenue Historic District. And of course, check out Cave Hollow West Winery, not just for the wine, but for the cheese—aged in Mark Twain Cave!

Events

Notable events in Hannibal include the Twain on Main Festival, Rotary Riverfest, Juneteenth Celebration, Tom Sawyer Days, Big River Steampunk Festival, Harvest Hootenanny Festival, Folklife Festival, and Mark Twain Birthday Bash.

Vitals / Fun Facts

- By 1860, Hannibal was the second-largest city and third-largest commercial center in the state.
- The *Tom & Huck* statue—a well-known Hannibal landmark—is one of the earliest known monuments to fictional characters, erected in 1926.

Rockcliffe Mansion is one of Hannibal's finest historic homes.
Courtesy of the Library of Congress

HERMANN

Gasconade County — Population 2,185

Founding Story

If you're a fan of Missouri wine you've no doubt heard of—or maybe even visited—Hermann, Missouri, but this town is so much more than its wineries. Hermann is Missouri's own little slice of Germany in the heartland, thanks to the vision of the town's original settlers. When word spread about the Missouri River Valley's resemblance to the Rhine Valley, members of the German Settlement Society of Philadelphia were intrigued, and sent scouts to see for themselves and ideally choose a place for a new colony that could be "German in every particular." The land for the town was chosen in 1837, which at the time was steep, rugged, rocky terrain along the Missouri River. The view was stunning, but the land? Not as much. But the German settlers persevered, and used the rocky hills to plant vineyards that would eventually lead to Hermann's success as a major winery destination, beginning with the establishment of Stone Hill Winery in 1847.

Hermann has a fascinating Civil War history, most notably with the abolitionist cause, as many Germans believed they could not support enslavement here in America when they themselves had fled persecution and harsh conditions in their homeland. Though Missouri was a battleground state, many German immigrants fought with the Union Army and were an important asset to their cause.

After the war, Hermann flourished. Hermann's settlers designed the town's street system to model that of Philadelphia, with a wide main street and grid, and filled the downtown avenues with businesses, taverns, warehouses, and more to support the growing community. Today, Hermann is home to over 150 buildings placed on the National Register of Historic Places, plus Missouri's oldest winery and the longest continuously running tavern in the state, just a sampling of the rich history and traditions in this community. The town is a highly sought-after destination with visitors from around the world traveling to mid-Missouri to experience this vibrant community with rich German cultural heritage woven throughout the town's architecture, events, and businesses.

The Strehly House provides a look at the lifestyle of a modest German family in Hermann.
Courtesy of Deutschheim Verein

The Gasconade County Courthouse overlooking the railroad and the Missouri River
Courtesy of Cultural Landscape Foundation

Hermann is one of the most picturesque small towns in Missouri.
Courtesy of Experience Hermann

Legends
William H. Pommer and his family moved to Hermann from Philadelphia and were known for manufacturing musical instruments, most prominently pianos. Pommer became a composer and later the founding dean of the University of Missouri School of Music.

Lore
Germans in Missouri largely supported the Union during the Civil War. Two were Carl Strehly and his brother-in-law, Edward Muehl, who published a German language newspaper in the basement of the Strehly House called the *Hermanner Wochenblatt*. In 1853, the press began printing copies of *Uncle Tom's Cabin* in German and continued to print it weekly for 26 weeks. As the country suffered leading up to and during the Civil War, the men began publishing abolitionist articles in their paper, with Muehl quoted as saying, "We did not escape oppression in our old homeland to support it here in America."

Stone Hill Winery was once the second-largest vineyard in the United States prior to Prohibition.
Courtesy of Stone Hill Winery

Attractions
Visit Deutschheim State Historic Site, comprising the Pommer-Gentner House, a period-appropriate Gemusegarten ("kitchen garden"), and the Strehly House, to learn about daily life for different German families in the town. For more history, check out the Historic Hermann Museum, enjoy both wine and history at Stone Hill Winery, stroll and shop the Hermann Historic District, and of course, indulge in award-winning German food at Hermann Wurst Haus.

Hermann's Historic District is home to restaurants, antiques, and shops.
Courtesy of Legends of America

Events

If you're looking for German cultural events, look no further! Head to Hermann for its annual Wurstfest, Maifest, Oktoberfest, and Christkindl Markt.

Vitals / Fun Facts

- Hermann has more than 150 sites listed on the National Register of Historic Places.
- The clock of the bell tower in the Hermann School (now the Historic Hermann Museum) is still wound by hand by its dedicated volunteers.
- The Concert Hall and Barrel Tavern is the oldest continuously operated tavern west of the Mississippi River (built in 1878).

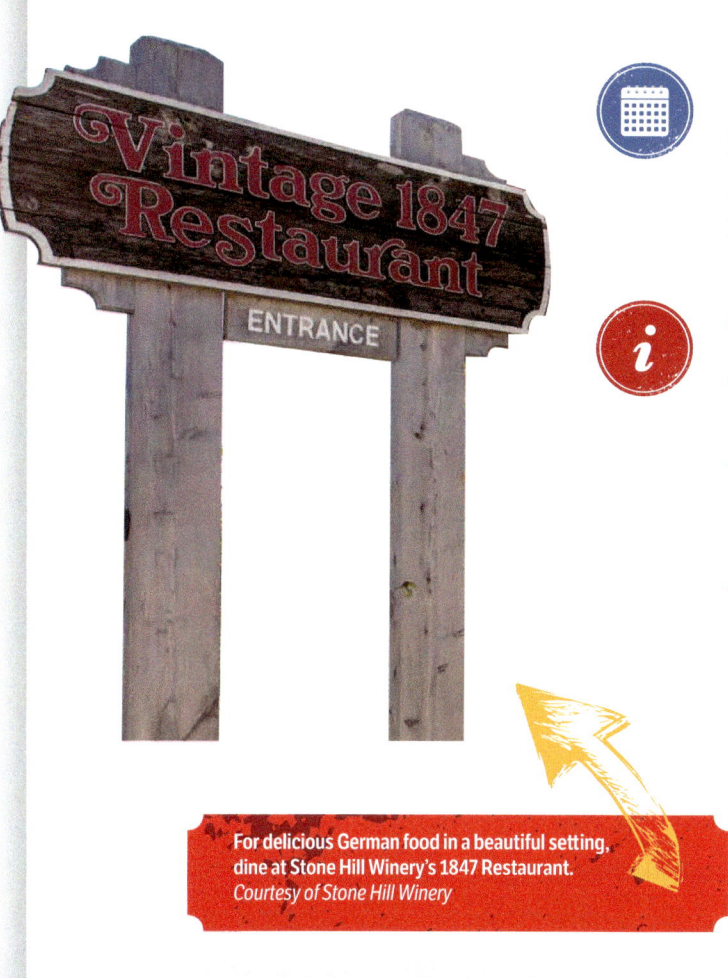

For delicious German food in a beautiful setting, dine at Stone Hill Winery's 1847 Restaurant.
Courtesy of Stone Hill Winery

Barrels of Missouri wine in the cellars of Stone Hill Winery await visitors to enjoy!
Courtesy of Stone Hill Winery

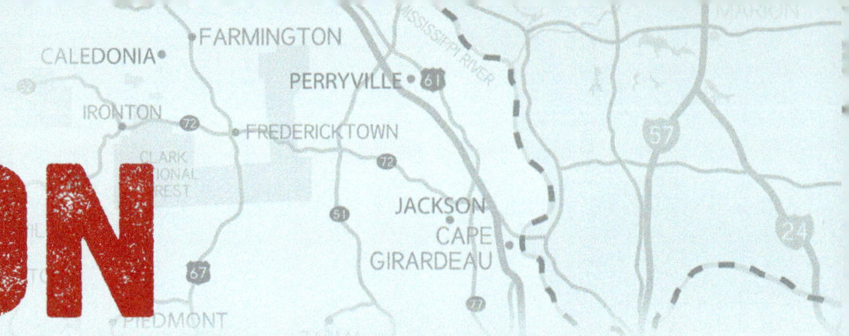

JACKSON

Cape Girardeau County
POPULATION
15,481

Founding Story

Come to Jackson and bask in over 200 years of history, which can be felt all over this Southeast Missouri town. Founded in 1815, Jackson was named for Andrew Jackson after his recent military victory over the British at the Battle of New Orleans. At one time, the growth of Jackson rivaled that of nearby Cape Girardeau, but the coming of the steamboats on the Mississippi River propelled Cape Girardeau to a higher population and faster industry growth. However, Jackson continued to grow and was still commercially successful, with many businesses, milling companies, and farms—in addition to the Iron Mountain Railroad—contributing to a robust economy and progressive community. Today, Jackson is thriving and hosts many community events throughout the year to entertain all ages. If you're a fan of history or exploring the outdoors, the town's historic buildings, museums, and two nearby state parks combine these perfectly.

The McKendree Chapel, built in 1819, was in deep neglect by the early 1900s, but preservation efforts in the mid-20th century saved this piece of Jackon history.
Courtesy of Old McKendree Chapel

Legends

Marie Watkins Oliver, called the "Betsy Ross of Missouri," lived in Jackson. She is credited with designing and creating the Missouri state flag. You can visit her home in Jackson, the Oliver House Museum.

Marie Watkins Oliver
Courtesy of the State Historical Society of Missouri

Lore

Jackson was once known throughout Southeast Missouri as "Old Jackson," a commentary on the town's reputation for "degradation and rowdyism." Around the turn of the century, fights and other disorderly conduct were more common than not in Jackson, but as industry in the area began to grow more rapidly, the attitudes and behaviors in town shifted.

Bollinger Mill was once used to grind wheat and corn.
Courtesy of Missouri State Parks

Attractions

During your visit to Jackson, visit Trail of Tears State Park, Bollinger Mill State Historic Site, Maintz Wildlife Preserve, Cape Girardeau Conservation Nature Center, Cape Girardeau County History Center, Old McKendree Chapel, Knowlan Family Farm, Riverside Regional Library, and Cape Safari Park, and spend some time traversing historic Uptown Jackson.

Jackson City Park is popular for weddings and family events.
Courtesy of Jackson Tourism

Events

Jackson hosts a variety of events and activities throughout the year, such as its weekly summer concerts, annual Oktoberfest, Arts/Crafts/Collections & Musical Festival, Rockin' the Garden Concert Series, themed train rides, Jackson in Bloom, Homecomers fair, and Christmas parade.

The Cape County Courthouse in Jackson is a perfect example of the beauty of small-town courthouses in Missouri.
Courtesy of Ken Steinhoff

Vitals / Fun Facts

- Jackson was the first community in the United States to be named for Andrew Jackson, which was done before he was even president.
- Jackson was selected by CNN's Money magazine in 2011 as the 59th best small town in the United States in which to live.

JAMESPORT

Daviess County
POPULATION
559

Founding Story

Jamesport was first settled in 1858, and it seemed there could be no better place to settle. The land was fertile, the views were breathtaking, and the area was growing. At the start, Jamesport's growth was slow for a time, but as the railroads began to develop and extend their lines in the late 19th century, Jamesport built up their industry and commerce to accommodate them. Into the 20th century, the community started to experience some significant cultural and economic shifts. Though Missouri has several towns with active Amish communities, Amish families began to set up homesteads in Jamesport in the 1950s because the land was affordable and available, and they were able to keep their families close. Today, Jamesport is Missouri's largest Amish settlement and is home to the largest community of Old Order Amish west of the Mississippi. Visitors to Jamesport today fill their time exploring many unique shops and businesses, enjoying delicious food (both sweet and savory!), and admiring the beautiful scenery.

Jamesport is home to a large population of Old Order Amish who have greatly influenced the culture and economy of the community.
Courtesy of Bryan Stalder/Kansas City Northeast News

Jamesport embraces the contributions of the Amish community.
Courtesy of Stephen Conn

Legends

Martha Scott, Academy Award-nominated actress, known for films such as Cecil B. DeMille's *The Ten Commandments*, William Wyler's *Ben-Hur*, and both the stage and film productions of Thornton Wilder's *Our Town*, was born in Jamesport and spent most of her childhood there.

Lore

Jamesport is a town that history seemingly tried to forget. During the 1870 census, official records failed to mention that the town still existed, when in fact it had doubled in population from 59 to about 120 residents.

Attractions

Be sure to visit the variety of antique stores in Jamesport, as well as the many Amish businesses such as the greenhouses, country stores, furniture stores, and creamery. The town has several places to eat and drink, and quaint, cozy lodging options, as well.

Downtown Jamesport has a variety of restaurants, shops, bakeries, and more to explore.
Courtesy of Premier Travel Media

Start your day right with a cup of coffee and something sweet to energize you for your Jamesport adventure!
Courtesy of Gingerich Dutch Pantry

Jamesport celebrates its story at the annual Heritage Days festival.
Courtesy of Remax Kansas and Missouri

Events

Jamesport has lots of community events and activities each year, including its Toy Tractor Show and May Days Festival in the spring; a Wine Walk, Freedom Festival, and Jamesport Livestock Fair and Parade in the summer; and its Heritage Days and Quilt Show in the fall. It also celebrates the holiday season with its annual Christmas Festival and hosts community fish fries seasonally.

Vitals / Fun Facts

- Originally, seven Amish families settled in Jamesport, and that has since grown to more than 175 families.

KEYTESVILLE

Chariton County
POPULATION 440

Founding Story

Keytesville's story begins with the small village of "Old Chariton," a modest town on the Missouri and Chariton Rivers that was the center of activity for the county for quite some time. However, the town was prone to frequent flooding, and the need arose to move the community to higher ground. An Englishman named James Keyte donated 50 acres of his land to Chariton County, and the town was officially established as Keytesville in 1833 and named in his honor. Keyte also built the first home and established the first business in the new Keytesville. The community built a courthouse and added more businesses like a hotel, distillery, and restaurants. Keytesville didn't have the advantage of being a railroad depot, and the closest was over a mile outside of town. To provide better access to the railroad for the community, a streetcar was built to transport goods and passengers to and from Keytesville and the depot. As many small towns experienced over time, the community's population decreased in the later 20th and into the 21st century, but Keytesville remains a close-knit community with several tourist attractions, a strong agricultural industry, and many successful businesses.

Park Street Historic Complex is the perfect spot to take a step back in time.
Courtesy of Friends of Keytesville

Legends

Gen. Maxwell D. Taylor, commander of the 101st Airborne "Screaming Eagles" during D-Day and the Battle of Normandy, and later Army chief of staff and then chairman of the Joint Chiefs of Staff, is from Keytesville. Confederate Gen. Sterling Price, known throughout Missouri for "Price's Raid" during the Civil War, is also from the area and has personal artifacts in the local museum.

Lore

Many of the water scenes from the 1973 film *Tom Sawyer* were filmed nearby at Dalton's Cut-Off Lake, particularly scenes that featured Huck and Tom's adventures on the Missouri River.

Attractions

Visit Maxwell Taylor Park, the Park Street historic complex, and the Price Museum; dine at 1820 Restaurant; hop over to nearby Brunswick to see the World's Largest Pecan; and for some time with nature, head to Hubert Conservation Area and Dalton Bottoms Access.

Events

Keytesville hosts its annual Bridge Street Affair, Sterling Price Days, and Dalton Days Festival. Its neighbor, Brunswick, has a fun Pecan Festival each year, as well.

Vitals / Fun Facts

- Keytesville's old town jail was commonly referred to as "the calaboose," which is a Spanish term for "little dungeon." It was mainly used as a place to hold the drunk and disorderly.
- The Dalton Vocational School is called the Tuskegee of the Midwest. It was founded in 1907 by Nathanial Bruce, a student of Booker T. Washington.

In neighboring Brunswick, the annual Pecan Festival draws crowds from near and far.
Courtesy of City of Brunswick

To commune with nature, spend some time at Dalton Bottoms Access.
Courtesy of Missouri Department of Conservation

The Barbagallo House is one of several historic homes that have been lovingly preserved and restored in town.
Courtesy of Future Expat

KIMMSWICK

Founding Story

The town of Kimmswick is a true Missouri gem, with activities, events, and sites to please even the choosiest of travelers. Kimmswick was founded in 1859 by Theodore Kimm, and it's likely he named the town by combining his last name and the name of his homeland, Brunswick, Germany. Kimm was a merchant, and he and other settlers were instrumental in a fast-growing community that had a mill, a brewery, a brickyard, a copper shop, a wagon maker, a blacksmith shop, and other shops established in town by 1867. The town flourished for the next century for its proximity to the Mississippi River and the railroad, and was an early tourist attraction thanks to showboats that would stop in town on the river and an amusement park that housed mineral springs and other entertainment.

The town experienced a period of decline in the mid 1900s with the popularity of automobiles and the slowing of trains and riverboats, but in a few decades that would all change. When the heir to the 7UP fortune, Lucianna Gladney Ross, visited Kimmswick and saw the town's deterioration, she pledged to help bring it back to its former glory. Ross's advocacy and funding assistance aided major restoration and revitalization efforts in Kimmswick.

Interest in the area continued to grow with the establishment of Mastodon State Park, which began as an archaeological and paleontological site where the bones of mastodons and other extinct animals were found in the 19th century, and it became one of the most extensive Pleistocene ice age sites in the world. The area was threatened when Highway 55 construction began, and was purchased by the state of Missouri to preserve and share with its people.

Thanks to the preservation efforts of many, Kimmswick flourished as shops, restaurants, and historic sites gained popularity with tourists and residents alike. Today, in this small Missouri town of under 200 people, there are now over two dozen restaurants and businesses for visitors to experience.

Jefferson County — **POPULATION 133**

The Blue Owl Restaurant and Bakery is world-famous for its Levee High Apple Pie.
Courtesy of Gregg Goldman | Explore St. Louis

Legends

Fred Anheuser, former vice president of Anheuser-Busch and grandson of the beer baron himself, and his wife, Mabel-Ruth Anheuser, had an estate in Kimmswick. Fred was the last Anheuser to lead the company, and after his death, Mabel and their heirs left the estate to the city of Kimmswick. The city offers tours of the home and grounds, which pay homage to the contributions of the family to Kimmswick and the St. Louis region.

Lore

Lucianna Gladney Ross, heir to the 7UP fortune, once visited the area in the 1970s and was disheartened by the state of Kimmswick. The dilapidated buildings, especially in such a historical and beautiful downtown district, inspired her to act, and Ross led major revitalization efforts in the town. She is credited with "saving Kimmswick."

Families flock to Mastadon State Park during the warmer months to explore the trails and wade in the cool spring-fed creek.

A carved tree trunk welcomes guests for the annual Apple Butter Festival.
Courtesy of Future Expat

Attractions

Perhaps one of the most popular spots in Kimmswick is the Blue Owl Restaurant & Bakery, home of the Levee High Apple Pie. After you indulge, peruse the beautiful downtown shops; enjoy scenic views of the Mighty Mississippi; or head to Mastodon State Park for some intriguing history, peaceful trails, and spring-fed creeks.

Events

The two biggest Kimmswick events each year are the Apple Butter Festival in the fall and the Strawberry Festival in the spring. You won't want to miss them!

Vitals / Fun Facts

- Kimmswick is home to the oldest known wrought-iron bridge in Missouri, the Windsor Harbor Road Bridge, constructed in 1874 and now listed on the National Register of Historic Places.

The Windsor Harbor Road Bridge is the oldest-known wrought iron bridge in the state, constructed in 1874.
Courtesy of Go Kimmswick

Mastodon State Park's interpretive center is full of some colossal exhibits!
Courtesy of Mastodon State Park

The Kimmswick Apple Butter Festival (pictured here) and Strawberry Festival are two of the area's most popular events.
Courtesy of Small Batch Winery

Kimmswick was a crucial port along the Mississippi River for the transportation of goods.
Courtesy of Go Kimmswick

KIRKSVILLE

Adair County
POPULATION
17,530

Founding Story

Though most recognized for its universities and popular state park, Kirksville also provides visitors with rich history, intriguing stories, and plenty of sites to explore. Kirksville's origin story begins with its early settlers, many of whom came from Kentucky, who established Adair County and named this new community as the county seat in 1841. According to local legend, the name for the town comes from an evening with early settler and tavern owner Jesse Kirk, who traded a Thanksgiving dinner and good whiskey for the town's naming rights. Kirksville has a rich history and is most known as the location of the Civil War Battle of Kirksville, and for being the home of Truman State University. Today, the town serves as a cultural, economic, and educational hub for the region. Plan a visit and discover why Kirksville is called "Missouri's North Star."

Legends

Dr. Andrew Taylor Still (commonly referred to as A. T. Still), the founder of osteopathic medicine, established the world's first osteopathic medical school in Kirksville: A. T. Still University.

Academy Award, Golden Globe, and Emmy Award-winning actress Geraldine Page was born and spent part of her childhood in Kirksville.

Kirksville's quaint downtown has seen a lot of growth in the past several years with new businesses and building preservation.
Courtesy of Truman Media Network

Lore

Popular lore in Kirksville is the story of the Devil's Chair in Highland Park Cemetery. The legend says that if any person sits on the chair at midnight or on Halloween night, a hand from below ground will pull the person underground to the depths of hell.

Attractions

Thousand Hills State Park is a popular spot for outdoor recreation. Kirksville is full of places for the history lover, including the Adair County Historical Society Museum, Ruth Towne Museum and Visitors Center, Kirksville Historic Site audio tour, and the Museum of Osteopathic Medicine. Also, check out the seasonal Kiwanis farmers' market on the town square.

Williard Hotel
Courtesy of Kirksville Daily Express

Events

There are many great events in Kirksville throughout the year, such as the Kirksville Art Walk; performances at Curtain Call Theatre; the Summer on the Square concert series; the Red, White, and Blue Festival; the NEMO Fair; and the Red Barn Arts and Crafts Festival. In addition, Truman State University puts on several concerts, theater performances, and other events throughout the year.

Truman State University began in 1867 and has helped Kirksville become an economic and educational hub of Northeastern Missouri.
Courtesy of Truman State University

Catch the Kiwanis Farmers Market seasonally on Saturday mornings on the Kirksville downtown square for local produce and handmade goods.
Courtesy of KTVO

Vitals/Fun Facts

- Kirksville translates to "village of churches," from the Scottish word "kirk" for "church," but the town has no known significant connection to Scotland or Scottish settlers. Even so, the town hosts an annual Scottish Highland Games, with traditional competitions.
- The Adair County Historical Society Museum has in its collections the cannonball that hit the courthouse during the Civil War's Battle of Kirksville.
- Enjoy pancakes? What about more than 15 different kinds of pancakes? If this sounds delectable, then head to Pancake City.

LAMAR

Barton County
POPULATION
4,266

Founding Story

So much history is steeped into this southwest Missouri town, and the community is eager to share its story. Lamar was settled in 1856. At first, the town was incorporated into Jasper County, but once Barton County was formed, Lamar was named the county seat of the new county. The town was named for the president of what was then the Republic of Texas—Mirabeau Lamar—who was a friend of one of Lamar's founders. It experienced significant hardships during the Civil War, with the town experiencing multiple attacks due to its location near the Missouri–Kansas border. However, most people who know Lamar know it for its title as the birthplace of our 33rd president, Harry S. Truman, the only US president to hail from Missouri. In the 20th century, the town grew to be a thriving agricultural community with state and national historical significance, and today boasts the second largest city square in the state.

The birthplace of Harry S. Truman has been meticulously preserved and stands in homage to the 33rd president of the United States.

Legends
Lamar is the birthplace of President Harry S. Truman. It is also where Wyatt Earp—arguably most known for his involvement in the legendary gunfight at the OK Corral—began his career as a lawman as the town's first constable.

Lore
Lamar as it is today almost never came to be. The town was burned during the Missouri-Kansas Border War (1854-1859) and again during the Civil War in 1864, and then the town was almost depopulated. Slow but steady growth due to agriculture and small business helped re-establish the area.

Attractions
Lamar is fortunate to have many great sites, including of course the Harry S. Truman Birthplace National Historic Site. Catch a football game to watch the legendary state champions at Lamar High School. To spend time in nature, head to Prairie State Park. The Stilabower Public Observatory is one of only four community-owned observatories in the United States.

Events
Celebrate with Lamar at its annual Truman Day, Lamar Free Fair, and Fallfest, or attend high school football tailgates to get a real feel for Lamar spirit.

Vitals/Fun Facts
- Lamar went through four courthouses in its first 30 years.
- Lamar calls itself "a place of legendary beginnings," largely because of its historical significance with Harry S. Truman and Wyatt Earp.

Athletics at Lamar High School have given the community something to rally around, which has created positive change in the town.
Courtesy of Missouri Humanities

Battle of Lexington
Courtesy of Missouri Historical Society

LEXINGTON

Founding Story

Lexington is a popular spot to visit here in the Show-Me state for Civil War buffs, but there's a lot more to this town's story that makes Lexington worthy of a visit. The town began as a ferry landing on the Missouri River in 1822 and became the county seat of Lafayette County, which was formerly called Lillard County, the following year. River commerce helped the town prosper quickly in its beginning years, and during the 1830s and '40s, the town was the largest city west of St. Louis.

Dry goods stores, inns, blacksmiths, and taverns were opened in town to service travelers heading westward along the Sante Fe, Oregon, California, and Mormon Trails, and soon, the use of steamboats became popular and coal mines were dug in the bluffs surrounding Lexington to aid the enterprise. Smaller communities in the area would also use Lexington as a port, selling and distributing their goods along the bustling riverway.

The strategic location and economic prosperity of the town made it an important city to protect during the Civil War, and two battles were fought in Lexington during the war. The first battle is known as the Battle of the Hemp Bales, which occurred in 1861, and the second was in 1864, part of Sterling Price's raid through Missouri. Both engagements ended in Union defeat, and guerilla warfare continued in the area even months after the official end of the Civil War.

These stories are preserved at the Battle of Lexington State Historic Site, which has grown to be a very popular tourist attraction in the area, as well as the Lexington Historical Society and the Wentworth Military Academy Museum. Visitors will also find historic districts, parks, restaurants, and wineries to enjoy during their stay in Lexington, providing a destination for travelers of all interests.

Lafayette County
POPULATION 4,652

Erected in 1925, this memorial honors veterans from foreign wars from Lafayette County.
Courtesy of Civil War Talk

Carl Stalling was born in Lexington and composed for both Walt Disney and Warner Brothers.
Courtesy of Houston Public Media

Legends
Many known names hail from Lexington. Arguably one of the most fascinating is Carl W. Stalling, born in Lexington, who composed and arranged some of the most memorable tunes for Bugs Bunny and other Warner Brothers cartoons, as well as early compositions with Walt Disney, beginning with the "Silly Symphonies" short films.

This stunning home is just one example of the many historic properties in the area.
Courtesy of City of Lexington

Lore
A section of town known as "Block 42" has remained an infamous piece of Lexington lore. It's said that this section of town had 42 saloons, brothels, and other "places men frequent" during the Prohibition area. During the 1930s and '40s, there were many bars on the block, and while the weekends saw much activity downtown for shopping and strolling, it's said that the men would go to these bars and involve themselves in dubious activities. Block 42 developed such a reputation that many families forbade their children from going to the area. Come to find out, it wasn't feasible to fit 42 businesses on a small downtown block, but it makes for some interesting stories.

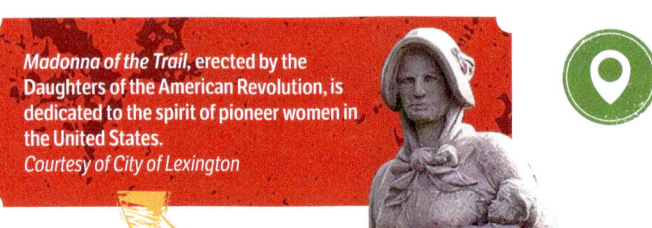
Madonna of the Trail, erected by the Daughters of the American Revolution, is dedicated to the spirit of pioneer women in the United States.
Courtesy of City of Lexington

Attractions
Lexington has no shortage of places to visit, including the Battle of Lexington State Historic Site, "The Cannonball" at the County Courthouse, a World War I memorial, Riverfront Park, Crystal Lake Park, and Lexington Historical Museum. Lexington also has four different historic districts and a local wine trail to explore.

Events

Lexington features a Fall Festival, Fine Arts and Photography Show, Christmas Bazaar and Craft Show, Lexington Community Fair, and performances at the Rainbow Ranch.

Vitals/Fun Facts

- A cannonball shot during the Battle of Lexington in 1861 is still lodged in and visible at the top of one of the pillars at the Lafayette County Courthouse.
- Guerilla warfare was still rampant in the area after the Civil War. One such incident led to a young Jesse James being shot and wounded in the lung. Some say this was a big reason he became a bank robber and outlaw in his later years.
- The Lafayette County Courthouse, built in 1847, is the oldest continuously used courthouse west of the Mississippi and is one of only two temple-style courthouses still in use as courthouses in Missouri.

Lexington is a destination for history lovers with museums, historic sites, and more.
Courtesy of City of Lexington

LOUISIANA

Pike County
POPULATION 3,199

Founding Story

Louisiana is one of many towns that owes its early growth and success to the Mississippi River. Founded in 1816, the town of Louisiana is believed to have been named for the daughter of an early settler of the town, who is supposedly the first child born in St. Louis after the Louisiana Purchase of 1803. The town became a bustling port city within only a couple of decades because of its location, with river commerce keeping the port busy. Louisiana saw a lot of trading and transportation, and growth continued as the railroad came through the area in the 1870s. The town saw decline as other towns in the area continued to grow, and it suffered from numerous floods over the years. However, the quaint downtown, beautiful river views, and wildlife started attracting more people to visit in recent years, and preservation efforts are alive and well in Louisiana.

Louisiana is a top destination for watching bald eagles along the river.
Courtesy of Great River Road

Historic downtown Louisiana is just steps away from the Mighty Mississippi, so visitors can enjoy both the quaint streets and the scenic river views.
Courtesy of Eagles Nest B&B

Legends

Former Missouri governor Lloyd Stark called Louisiana home, as well as MLB player and later broadcaster Jack Graney. John Brooks Henderson had a beautiful home in Louisiana, which still stands; he was the US senator who proposed the original bill that eventually led to the 13th amendment abolishing slavery in the United States.

Lore

In the 1890s, Stark Brothers Nurseries & Orchards was introduced to a mysterious variety of apple during a contest for new apple varieties. The apple was more elongated than others and had five bumps on the bottom. It was named the Red Delicious apple, and Stark Brothers quickly purchased the rights to it, followed soon after by the sweeter Golden Delicious apple. These two varieties are the ancestors of more than 60 percent of the world's apples.

Attractions

Traverse the stunning Victorian streetscapes and visit the Louisiana Area Historical Museum and Stark Brothers Nurseries and Orchards—the world's oldest continuously operating nursery. Louisiana is also part of the 50 Miles of Art corridor, comprising Hannibal, Louisiana, and Clarksville.

Events

Visitors flock (no pun intended) to Louisiana every year for some of the best eagle watching in the state. For some beautiful architecture, take the Great Mansions and Estates Tour or have a blast at the Louisiana Country Colorfest.

Vitals/Fun Facts

- The Missouri Department of Natural Resources states that Louisiana has the most intact Victorian streetscape in Missouri.

Louisiana offers stunning views of the Mississippi River.
Courtesy of Great River Road

MANSFIELD

Wright County
POPULATION 1,193

Founding Story

Mansfield is a retreat for anyone seeking unique places and rich history set among the calm serenity of rural Missouri. The land for what was to become Mansfield was purchased to service the railroad, and the town was established in 1881. Mansfield's beginnings included the railroad depot, a church, post office, and a school, but it soon saw rapid growth from the mining industry in the area. By the 1890s, Mansfield was the fastest growing community in the county. However, the community's early success could not stop the inevitable economic turmoil during the 20th century. The town declined beginning in the 1920s as the mining boom cooled down, and was not immune to the effects of the Great Depression. Mansfield struggled for many years to build back its population and economy. However, tourism helped revive the community when the Laura Ingalls Wilder home opened to the public, and the site now draws international attention for how successfully Mansfield has preserved the community's stories and places.

In addition to being a top producer of heirloom seeds, Baker Creek maintains Bakersville Pioneer Village.
Courtesy of Brandon Alms

Laura Ingalls Wilder and her husband, Almanzo, settled just outside Mansfield in 1894 at Rocky Ridge Farm, where Laura wrote her famed books and they both lived out the rest of their lives.
Courtesy of the State Historical Society of Missouri

Legends
Laura Ingalls Wilder, author of the acclaimed Little House book series, moved here with her husband and daughter in 1894 and wrote her famed books about her family's pioneer life at her home in Mansfield.

Lore
A book by William Holtz, *The Ghost in the Little House*, chronicles the life of Laura Ingalls Wilder's daughter, Rose. It also makes the claim that Rose is actually the ghostwriter of the Little House series, though this has not been proven.

Attractions
Of course, visit the Laura Ingalls Wilder Historic Home and the Laura Ingalls Wilder-Rose Wilder Lane Museum, check out Baker Creek Heirloom Seeds and its amazing pioneer village, and explore Cedar Gap Conservation Area to see Cedar Gap Plateau, the second-highest point in Missouri.

Baker Creek Pioneer Village
Courtesy of Brandon Alms

Events
Make the trip to Mansfield for the annual Wilder Days Festival in September and check out performances by the Ozark Mountain Players theater group throughout the year.

Vitals / Fun Facts
- Mansfield was named by the Smithsonian as one of the top 15 small towns to visit in 2023.
- Butter Day has celebrated the dairy industry annually since 1953.
- The beautiful barn that houses the Laura Ingalls Wilder-Rose Wilder Lane Museum holds the largest Ingalls-Wilder collection in the world.

Mansfield is a community that loves to come together for a cause and celebrate the town's rich history.
Courtesy of City of Mansfield

MARCELINE

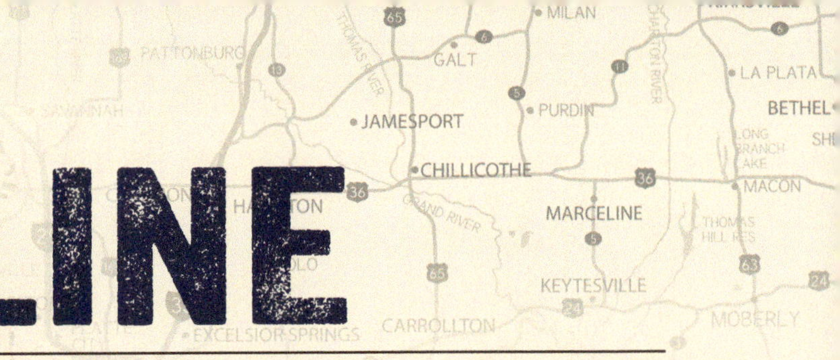

Chariton/Linn Counties
POPULATION 2,123

Founding Story

Another Highway 36 "Way of American Genius" community worthy of a trip is the community of Marceline. A railroad town through and through, Marceline was founded by the Sante Fe railroad in 1888 to serve as a terminal between Chicago and Kansas City. The Sante Fe railroad was the first to establish a direct rail line between these two booming midwestern cities, making Marceline's role an important one in the rich rail commerce and transportation history in Missouri. The town was named after Marcelina, the wife of one of the railroad directors, and was a lively, steady community. Several industries thrived in Marceline's history, including printing, publishing, agriculture, and coal mining. The town has made great strides to tell its story and attract both residents and tourists to its idyllic community, which has a prominent downtown district with restaurants, museums, antique shops, and parks for all to enjoy.

When Disney moved to California, he built a replica of the barn on his home farm in Marceline. Marceline later used these blueprints to reproduce the barn to celebrate his 100th birthday.
Courtesy of Walt Disney Hometown Museum

Legends
Marceline is the boyhood home of the one and only Walt Disney. You may have heard of him.

Lore
Mining became an important industry in Marceline with the development of the railroad. However, before they could excavate mines, the miners had to grapple with a particular superstition: that luck would come if the first spadeful of earth was dug and thrown by a lady. So the wife of one of the promoters did the honor, and the mine shaft was named Lillian Shaft No. 1 in her honor.

Attractions
While in Marceline, head to the Walt Disney Hometown Museum and visit Walt's Dreaming Tree and Barn. Learn about Marceline's story on a self-guided walking tour, check out Marceline Carnegie Library, and spend some time outdoors at Walt Disney Municipal Park. For a little treat, head to Ma Vic's Corner Café for a "Dusty Miller," the town's signature ice cream dish made with vanilla ice cream, chocolate and marshmallow syrups, and malt powder.

The Walt Disney Hometown Museum connects visitors to the life and legacy of Disney.
Courtesy of Fox 4

Events
Some of the town's notable events include the Marceline City Market, Patriotic Pie War, Wine and Art Stroll, Peanut Night, and the Marceline Car and Train Show.

Vitals/Fun Facts
- The Main Street USAs in Disney World and Disneyland are modeled after Main Street (now Kansas Avenue) in Marceline.
- In Marceline, Disney saw his first stage production, *Peter Pan*, which he later turned into an animated feature film.
- The first graduating class of Marceline High School had only three students.

Disney saw his first stage production, which inspired a movie adaptation, in Marceline, and his hometown also inspired his love of trains.
Courtesy of Walt Disney Hometown Museum

MARSHFIELD

Webster County
POPULATION
7,458

Founding Story

Natural beauty and fascinating stories await visitors to Marshfield, located in Southwest Missouri. The first European settlers in the area came in the 1830s, but the town was not officially named until 1856. At that time, John McMahan named the county after Daniel Webster and the town after his hometown in Massachusetts. After the Civil War, the town grew rapidly because of the railroad, but the growth was short-lived. Less than 30 years after the town was established, a massive tornado ripped through the area and destroyed nearly the entire town. This disaster is still listed as one of the top 10 natural disasters in US history. But the town persisted and was rebuilt over time, and today Marshfield is popular for Route 66 enthusiasts and is celebrated for its annual events that draw visitors from far and wide. Most popular is Marshfield's annual Cherry Blossom Festival, a stunning sight and a must-see for any tourist looking to check off items on the Missouri bucket list.

Each year, Marshfield celebrates the coming of spring with the popular Cherry Blossom Festival.
Courtesy of Missouri Cherry Blossom Festival

Explore Hidden Waters Park for some picturesque scenery and peaceful time with nature.
Courtesy of City of Marshfield

Legends
Born here was Edwin P. Hubble, a groundbreaking (or should we say, "out of this world") astronomer and the namesake of the Hubble Space Telescope, our window into the universe.

Edwin P. Hubble
Courtesy of New Mexico Museum of Space History

Lore
Composer and Missourian John William "Blind" Boone composed a piece inspired by the 1888 tornado that destroyed Marshfield, aptly named "The Marshfield Cyclone." He chose this piece as his closing number at performances across the country, and it's said that the piece inspires the listener to experience the feelings of those who went through the disaster. However, we will never have the opportunity to hear it, as Boone refused to record the score, and it was last heard over 100 years ago at his final concert in Illinois.

Attractions
Learn about Missouri legends by traversing the Missouri Walk of Fame. For a stellar site, be sure to visit the Hubble telescope replica. Hidden Waters Nature Park is a great stop for anyone wanting a little slice of the peaceful outdoors, and if you're into history, Marshfield's Route 66 sites and the Webster County Historical Museum should be on your list!

Events
Visit Marshfield for events throughout the year, including the Cherry Blossom Festival, Webster County Fair, Independence Day Rodeo, Harvest Days, and Truck and Tractor Pull.

Vitals/Fun Facts
- In the early 1900s, the county exported nearly 50 percent of the state's tomatoes; by the 1920s, there were approximately 200 factories throughout the county.
- The aftermath of the infamous tornado included discovering multiple mineral springs, which then gained attention far and wide for their supposed healing abilities.

Marshfield uses murals to tell its story and add art and beauty to its downtown.
Courtesy of City of Marshfield

Several old grain elevators that once serviced the Katy Railroad have been purchased and painted with murals by local artist Bryan Haynes, known for his work depicting Missouri landscapes and heritage.
Courtesy of Magnificent Missouri

MARTHASVILLE

Warren County
POPULATION 1,245

The area that is now Marthasville was once part of the town of La Charette, an early Missouri settlement near the Missouri River. The community is noted in the journals of Lewis and Clark, where they reference La Charette as the last settlement they encountered before they headed west in 1804. The community is mentioned in their writings again during their return journey in 1806. The town of Marthasville was officially founded in 1817 and was the only official town in the county for over 10 years. It was a largely agricultural area, with rich farmland along the Missouri River Valley.

Over the next several decades, the population and economy grew as a result of an influx of German immigrants, who were influenced by German explorer Gottfried Duden. Duden came to what was then the western states of North America in the 1820s, and traversed much of the Missouri River Valley during his time. He wrote down his findings in his *Report on a Journey to the Western States of North America and A Stay of Several Years Along the Missouri (1825, '25, '26, and 1827)*. The book became popular back home, with many struck by Duden's descriptions of the Missouri River Valley resembling the Rhineland. Duden's writing is credited for inspiring thousands of German migrants to come to Missouri, and Marthasville became one such settlement.

The community's growth continued with the arrival of the Katy railroad, allowing farmers and merchants easy access to shipping their goods. Like other communities in the area, Marthasville saw decline after the Katy railroad left, leaving a void for commerce and transportation, but local wineries, historic sites, and soon the Katy Trail created a renewed interest in the community in the 1990s and into the 21st century.

Local historical societies, community groups, and passionate individuals are dedicated to preserving Marthasville's history and cultural heritage, and have done extensive work to share Marthasville's story through exhibits, community celebrations, and publications. The next time you're looking for Small Town America rich with history, beautiful scenery, and friendly people, give Marthasville a try!

Marthasville is located along the Katy Trail and is a popular spot to stop, take a rest, and enjoy the beautiful Missouri River Valley.
Courtesy of Justin Barr | St. Louis Magazine

Magnificent Missouri took over the Peers Store in 2014 and turned it into a Katy Trail visitors center, as well as transformed the landscape into a native prairie.
Courtesy of Magnificent Missouri

Marthasville, like many small towns in Missouri, thrived because of its agriculture industry.

Legends

Marthasville is called "The Last Home of Daniel Boone." Daniel Boone and his wife, Rebecca, moved to Marthasville when they were in their 60s and stayed with their children for the remainder of their lives. The only portrait of Daniel Boone that was painted from life was done in Marthasville in June 1820, just a few months before his death.

Lore

Rebecca Boone died in 1813 and was buried in the nearby family cemetery. Daniel Boone was buried with her upon his death in 1820. But there is disagreement and speculation over whether the graves are actually there. Supposedly, Boone's remains were exhumed in 1845 to be moved to a more prominent cemetery in Kentucky, but for many years, Marthasville claimed they dug up the wrong body. However, no one ever made attempts to prove the truth one way or the other, so memorials (or "graves," depending on what you believe) exist in both locations.

Native Plants at Peers Store Prairie

Attractions

Marthasville is a lovely stop along the Katy Trail, with places like the Peers Store, Grabs House, Daniel Boone Burial Site, Boone Monument Village, and Treloar Mercantile available to learn about the many stories and people of this area. Head a few miles down the road to Treloar to see the World's Largest Ear of Corn. Marthasville is also part of the Missouri Weinstrasse, so don't skip out on visiting some area wineries.

 ## Vitals/Fun Facts

- The Peers Store was once the Glosemeyer General Store, which was owned and operated by the Glosemeyer family (who still live in the area) from the 1890s until 2014.
- With the help of experts, the land between the Peers Store and the Katy Trail has been restored to a native prairie.

 ## Events

Catch live bluegrass music on the porch of the historic Peers Store and check out Marthasville's Summer Concert Series, Car and Bike Show, festivals and events at local wineries, concerts in the park, the annual Marthasville Heritage Celebration, and Sweet Corn Sunday in Treloar.

The Treloar Mercantile, just a few miles down Highway 94 from Marthasville, is a stunning example of a 19th-century country store.

Downtown Mexico provides boutiques, a massive quilt store, restaurants, antique shops, and more.
Courtesy of Mexico Chamber of Commerce

MEXICO

Founding Story

Many have surely passed signs for Mexico, Missouri, while driving the length of Highway 70, perhaps on the way to a Mizzou game or to hit up a weekend in Kansas City or St. Louis. Next time, consider getting off the highway and exploring the town!

Mexico and Audrain County's early history begins with settlers from Virginia, Kentucky, and Tennessee. A unique name for a community in the middle of Missouri, Mexico was so named because the town was established during a period of excitement for Texas, which was at the time attempting to gain independence from Mexico. Founded in 1837, the land comprising the original town consisted of woodlands, streams, and prairies. Early growth in Mexico was rather slow, with the local population mostly consisting of farmers, merchants, and their families for many years. More rapid town growth came with the establishment of the North Missouri railroad in 1856, one of the earliest railroad lines through the state.

Now equipped with a rail line, farmers and business owners had more opportunity for economic success, and more people sought out Mexico and the surrounding county to call home. The area saw a flurry of Civil War activity. In fact, the railroad was such an important asset that Union troops headquartered in Mexico for much of the war, including units led by general and eventual president Ulysses S. Grant, who was stationed in Mexico for a period of time.

Mexico continued to be an important agriculture community throughout the 19th and 20th centuries and played host to major manufacturing, most notably firebrick. These industries were an integral part of Mexico and Audrain County's economic vitality, and their successes earned them reputations for being a top producer of soybeans and biofuel, and the nickname "The Fire Brick Center of the World."

Mexico also developed into a key location for academia, as Hardin College for Young Ladies was established in 1873 and operated for 60 years, followed by the opening of the renowned Missouri Military Academy in 1889. The Missouri Military Academy has been acclaimed as a top private school in the nation, and its historic campus still bustles with students and visitors. Today, Mexico's thriving downtown square, inviting community events, and interesting historic sites make the town a great option for a weekend getaway in mid-Missouri.

Audrain County — POPULATION 11,460

This stunning home, known as Graceland, has been wonderfully preserved and is now home to the Audrain County Historical Society and Museum Complex.
Courtesy of 417 *Magazine*

Tyronn Lue
Courtesy of 93.9 The Eagle

Legends

A. P. Green founded Green Industries in Mexico, which manufactured fire-resistant clay bricks and remained a major employer in the area from the 1940s until the early 2000s. His grandson, Christopher "Kit" Bond, grew up in Mexico, became a two-term governor of Missouri, and represented Missouri in the US Senate for 24 years. In sports history, Mexico is the former home of former NBA player-turned-coach Tyronn Lue.

Lore

Rumor has it, Winston Churchill was supposed to have given his famous Iron Curtain speech in Mexico with A. P. Green, but he went to neighboring Fulton instead.

Murals like this help bring color and whimsy to Mexico's historic downtown square.
Courtesy of KXEO

Attractions

To learn about the area's rich history, head to Graceland, the Audrain County museum complex. Mexico is also home to the Missouri Military Academy, with its beautiful campus and historic buildings. The community has a vibrant downtown with lots of great shops, such as Kate's Hallmark Shop, Homestead Hearth quilting store, and numerous boutiques and antique shops. To view some of the most beautiful homes in the county, head to Green Estate Park, where the Green and Bond families' ancestral homes are located. (Please note: The park is public, but the homes are privately owned.)

Events

Some of Mexico's most well-known events are its annual Soybean Festival and its Walk Back in Time event at the Audrain County museum complex.

Vitals / Fun Facts

- Mexico is the biofuel capital of Missouri.
- General Ulysses S. Grant once visited the Graceland estate, which is now part of the Audrain County museum complex.

The Audrain County Museum Complex has several historic buildings and exhibits, including the old one-room schoolhouse built in 1903.
Courtesy of Audrain County Historical Society

Teal Lake provides a serene setting for a kayak or canoe ride and fishing.
Courtesy of Missouri Department of Conservation

Simmons' Stables was home to some of the finest saddlebred horses in the country. Today, the stables have been restored and serve as an event center.
Courtesy of KXEO

NEOSHO

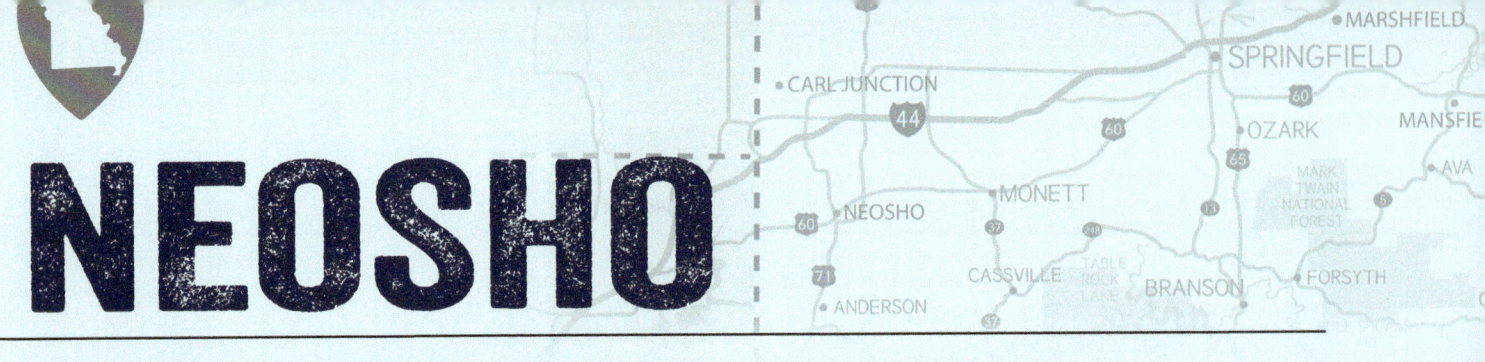

Newton County
POPULATION
13,061

Founding Story

In a community like Neosho, it's hard to know where to start exploring. With so many stories, places, and people that make this community unique, Neosho is a Missouri treasure. The land that is now the town of Neosho was first inhabited by the Osage, who used the many springs in the area for both ceremonial and practical reasons. White settlers of English, Irish, and Scottish ancestry began to settle the area in the 1830s, and Newton County was established in 1839 with Neosho as its county seat. The area was rich with natural resources and was attractive to those looking to settle somewhere with opportunity and promise. Commercial mining led to economic and population growth early on, which gained more traction with the coming of the railroad a few decades later. Successful shipping and manufacturing industries helped propel Neosho into the 20th century. The town is popular today for history buffs and outdoorsy folks alike for its variety of amenities and attractions, and a significant number of buildings in downtown Neosho are listed on the National Register of Historic Places.

Big Spring Park began in 1903 but the city didn't acquire the spring until 1927. The landscaping, bluffs, and spring provide a beautiful natural area for visitors to unwind.
Courtesy of City of Neosho

George Washington Carver
Courtesy of the National Park Service

Legends

Acclaimed American painter, muralist, and printmaker Thomas Hart Benton was born in Neosho. In addition, George Washington Carver was born in nearby Diamond, Missouri, but went to school in Neosho.

Lore

Nearby was born the legend of the Hornet Spook Light, a mysterious light phenomenon that was first seen in 1903 and was witnessed regularly by people for generations. Some local stories say the light is the ghost of a murdered Osage chief, or a Quapaw woman who tragically died after her warrior was killed in battle. Others think it's a more practical explanation, like headlights far in the distance or an odd reflection. No matter the explanation, the spooky story still draws attention more than 100 years later.

Attractions

The Neosho National Fish Hatchery is worth a visit as the oldest in the state, started in 1888. There's history aplenty during Newton County mural walking/driving tours, the Historic Downtown Neosho Walking Tour, the Longwell Museum at Crowder College, and the Newton County Historical Museum. While in the area, hop over to neighboring Diamond, Missouri, for the George Washington Carver National Monument to visit the birthplace of one of our nation's most important innovators.

Events

Check out the Thomas Hart Benton Festival, Celebrate Neosho event in the summer, fall festival, Dickens Christmas Faire, and annual Carver Day Festival.

Vitals/Fun Facts

- The name "Neosho" comes from the Osage language's "ne-o-zho" or "ne-u-zuh," meaning "clear or abundant water."
- Neosho is called Flower Box City and is home to the world's largest flower box.
- The area that is now Big Spring Park was once Indian trading grounds and later a Civil War camp.

The Neosho National Fishing Hatchery opened in 1888 and is the oldest fish hatchery in the state.
Courtesy of KSN16/KODE12

NEW HAVEN

Franklin County
POPULATION
2,414

Founding Story

New Haven is another example of a once-booming river town along the Missouri River that has put significant effort into showcasing its beautiful, historic riverfront and preserving its history. Founded in 1836, New Haven was originally named Miller's Landing because the town started with a steamboat landing on the Missouri River made by Philip Miller. Soon, German immigrants began settling the area as well, establishing farms and businesses. When construction of the Pacific Railroad reached Miller's Landing in 1855, steps were taken to formally establish the town, and the name changed to New Haven in 1856. River and railroad commerce kept the community growing for many decades, and businesses in town helped support these essential industries. Because of the town's deep roots and rich history, New Haven finds high importance in sharing the stories that helped shape the community. New Haven has become a destination for weddings and weekend getaways, with visitors drawn by its picturesque surroundings, bustling riverfront district, and small town hospitality.

Assumption Catholic Church is one of several historic churches in New Haven.
Courtesy of New Haven Chamber of Commerce

94 | SMALL TOWN MISSOURI

Legends

Explorer John Colter—often regarded as the first "mountain man"—settled in New Haven (then Miller's Landing) after his explorations and is buried here. Colter was part of Lewis and Clark's Corps of Discovery, but his personal claim to fame is his explorations during the winter of 1807-08. During this time, he became the first known person of European ancestry to see the Teton Range and explore what later became Yellowstone National Park. Colter Peak in Yellowstone is named for him.

Floating the Missouri River
Courtesy of Downtown New Haven Inc.

Lore

Author and former New Haven police officer Dan Terry—also known as Spookstalker Dan—is a ghost hunter. He has written several books on ghosts and other spooky tales around Missouri and has investigated many sites in and around New Haven for paranormal activity, of which he has found plenty.

Attractions

Explore the shops and historic buildings along the Riverfront District, and be sure to check out the John Colter Museum, the Old School, Ferry Boat Landing, and historic churches. Then, relax with a drink at Pinckney Bend Distillery or one of the many area wineries amid the beautiful rolling hills of the Missouri River Valley.

Events

Celebrate with New Haven at Balloon Fest, its Fall Festival, Scarecrow Festival and Pumpkin Glow, Christmas by Moonlight, and the Miller's Landing Day Festival.

New Haven honors John Colter with events and memorials in town. Colter is regarded as the first "mountain man" for his explorations out west.
Courtesy of New Haven Chamber of Commerce

Vitals/Fun Facts

- New Haven claims to be the place where Sun Drop soda was created in 1949.
- Tip: Stay at the Central Hotel for a bit of hospitality and history.

Downtown Pacific has retained its small-town charm.

PACIFIC

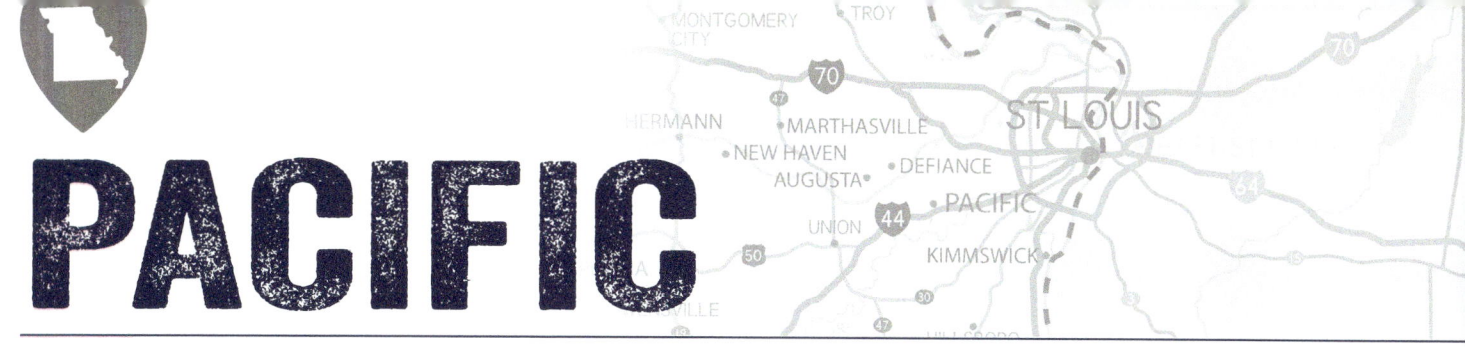

Founding Story

Though Pacific is just about 30 minutes west of the bustling city of St. Louis, the community has retained true small-town charm and amenities without succumbing to urban sprawl. Surrounded by nature preserves, conservation areas, and state parks, and equipped with plenty of attractions and lodging options, Pacific should make anyone's short list for a Missouri adventure.

The first log home in what would eventually become Pacific was built in 1820, but the town wasn't officially founded until 1852. The original name of the community was Franklin, and the town changed its name to Pacific several years later to honor the Atlanta-Pacific Railroad, which was completed through the town in 1853. The railroad helped the town thrive rather quickly, particularly as rail service began between St. Louis and Pacific in 1861.

The community suffered during the Civil War, and it was held by Confederate General Sterling Price until Union forces were dispatched to engage the Confederate troops. This battle led to a Union victory, which prevented Price from advancing his raid into St. Louis. Pacific's silica mining industry in the 1870s gave the town a much-needed economic boost and remains a prominent industry in the community today. Though the railroad and the Meramec River had already helped establish Pacific as a thriving and successful community, another asset was soon added.

A few decades into the 20th century, Route 66 was continued through Pacific, bringing cross-country travel and tourism to this small Missouri community that paved the way for more growing businesses to meet the demands of increased traffic. Route 66 remains a significant piece of Pacific's history that draws people to the community into the present day.

In recent years, Pacific gained another major tourist draw, when BIGFOOT 4x4 moved their headquarters from St. Louis to Pacific. Their garage is open to the public for tours, sharing the story of the original monster truck, and each year it hosts an open house that draws thousands of attendees and a line-up of thrilling monster truck events. Today, Pacific is excited to welcome visitors and proudly share the stories of their community and the importance of the "three Rs" as they call it—the river, the railroad, and Route 66—assets that make Pacific a place for history lovers, nature enthusiasts, and everything in between.

As you drive down historic Route 66 through Pacific, it's impossible to miss the large caves in the bluffs. Though not accessible to the public, these man-made caves represent Pacific's history as they date back over 150 years.
Courtesy of Jeffrey Lane

Legends

BIGFOOT 4x4, the first monster truck, is based in Pacific. The BIGFOOT team offers free tours of the facility and garage and hosts a free annual open house that showcases trucks and drivers from all over.

Lore

In October 1864, Confederate Gen. Sterling Price invaded Pacific and occupied the town. Union troops from St. Louis came in as reinforcements, and the two sides engaged in battle in the hills between Pacific and the nearby town of Allenton. The Union forces were victorious, which stopped Price's advance toward St. Louis. If not for this engagement in Pacific, the Civil War might have turned out very differently.

The Red Cedar Inn was a staple along Route 66 in Pacific and has recently been restored as a museum and visitors center.

Attractions

Start your Pacific adventure at the Red Cedar Inn Museum and Visitor Center on Route 66. Learn about the area's history, grab some maps and brochures, and get on your way! Of course, check out BIGFOOT, and if you're up for a challenge, walk the steps up to Jensen's Point for a stunning view of the area. If you want a beautiful view without the stairs, drive up to Blackburn Park for a peaceful picnic while taking in the scenery. Explore the many Route 66-era sites, or head to Shaw Nature Reserve or Purina Farms for more area attractions. For a unique place to stay, book a night or two at the Landing Hub or the Pacific Palace.

Events

Don't miss the annual BIGFOOT Open House and the Iron Horse Rodeo. Check out the Fall Fest at Red Cedar Inn and the seasonal farmers' market, as well.

Vitals/Fun Facts

- Pacific's big draws are referred to as the "Three Rs"—the river, the railroad, and Route 66, all three of which can be seen from Jensen's Point and Blackburn Park.
- As you drive along Route 66, you can't miss the several large caves in the bluffs. These were uncovered when Route 66 was realigned through Pacific and connected to Pacific's silica mining history, dating back over 150 years.

If the hike up to Jensen's Point isn't for you, never fear! Blackburn Park is accessible by vehicle and provides an equally breathtaking view of the town.
Courtesy of the Pacific Area Chamber of Commerce

The three Rs that are Pacific's lifeblood can be seen from above in one shot, providing a beautiful look at three facets of the community's story.
Courtesy of Missouri Humanities

You don't have to be a monster truck fan to know BIGFOOT. Credited as the first Monster Truck, the BIGFOOT Team is now headquartered in Pacific and is one of the most popular attractions.

Housed in a two-story home built in 1881, the Perry County Museum is dedicated to sharing the stories of the area's past.
Courtesy of Discover Lewis and Clark

PERRYVILLE

Founding Story

History runs deep in the Perryville area, and the communities in and around Perry County pride themselves on keeping the stories and places of their past alive. Perryville was organized as a community just before Missouri officially became a state in 1821, but the town wasn't incorporated until 1856. The community was named for Oliver Hazard Perry, a naval officer considered to be one of the great heroes of the War of 1812. Though originally part of Ste. Genevieve County, Perry County was soon established and Perryville named county seat.

The area was settled largely by German immigrants who began migrating to the area in the late 1830s and continuing into the 1870s. They established successful businesses and helped grow the population, and other surrounding communities like Frohna, Altenburg, and Brazeau also have deep German roots that are still celebrated today and remain an integral part of the area's cultural heritage and historical significance.

A popular attraction in Perryville is the Shrine of the Miraculous Medal. This grotto on the grounds is a serene place to rest and reflect.
Courtesy of St. Mary's Seminary

With two railroads arriving in Perryville—one in 1892 and one in 1904—the town's economy grew, helping the community's agricultural and commercial industries. During the town's first census count in 1860, the population was just over 300 people. Over the next 50 years, that number would grow to over 1,700 thanks to the thriving businesses and opportunities Perryville promised.

The area still celebrates its deep German roots, and examples of that German heritage can be seen throughout the county in its businesses, architecture, and events. One of the best examples of this heritage is the period log cabins and other buildings and living history at the Saxon Lutheran Memorial in nearby Frohna.

Interest in the community has grown in recent years, as Perryville was on the path of totality during both most recent total solar eclipses, and thousands had the chance to come to the town for the rare event and to explore Perryville. And while Missouri is renowned for its caves, many of these sought-after caves are found in Perry County, attracting spelunking enthusiasts from across the country. Adventure awaits in Perryville; the only issue will be figuring out how to fit everything in one trip!

Over the last several years, Perryville has brought hand-painted murals to its downtown buildings. The stunning paintings tell the town's story and add a fun element to the town square.
Courtesy of KFVS12

Legends

Hit country music singer-songwriter Chris Janson is from Perryville, and he frequently returns to perform and support his hometown.

Historic Structure at Saxon Lutheran Memorial
Courtesy of Saxon Lutheran Memorial

Lore

Tower Rock, located in the Mississippi River near the old Wittenburg town site, can be accessed by foot only when the river is at a very low point, and visitors from all over flock to Perry County when this happens. Plenty of lore surrounds Tower Rock, as it has been a well-known landmark and was documented by missionary and explorer Jacques Marquette in the 1600s and Lewis and Clark in the early 1800s. Native Americans warned Lewis and Clark that the water surrounding Tower Rock held demons. There are also ghost stories derived from river tragedies. Ghost story or not, the whirlpools that form around Tower Rock can be quite dangerous, so be mindful.

Attractions

What isn't there to do in Perryville? Places to put on your list include the National Shrine of Our Lady of the Miraculous Medal; American Tractor Museum; Old Appleton; Vietnam Veterans Memorial; nearby German communities of Frohna, Altenburg, Biehle, and Brazeau; the Lutheran Heritage Center; the Barn Quilt Trail; Saxon Lutheran Memorial; Ball Mill Resurgence Natural Area; Historic Faherty House; Perry County Military History Museum; and Perry County Museum, and you can't miss the stunning murals throughout town.

Events

When planning your trip, note the Christmas Country Church Tour, 573 Film Festival, Annual Seminary Picnic (124 years and counting), Mayfest, Saxon Lutheran Memorial Fall Festival, and caving classes.

Vitals/Fun Facts

- Perry County is home to 667 recorded limestone caves.
- The Vietnam Veterans Memorial in Perryville is an exact replica of the monument by Maya Lin in Washington, DC.
- Old Appleton Bridge that connects Perry and Cape Girardeau Counties is the only iron bridge in Missouri still in its original location.

Perryville is another example of a historic downtown square centered on a beautiful historic courthouse.
Courtesy of Ken Steinhoff

Saxon Lutheran Memorial Complex
Courtesy of Saxon Lutheran Memorial

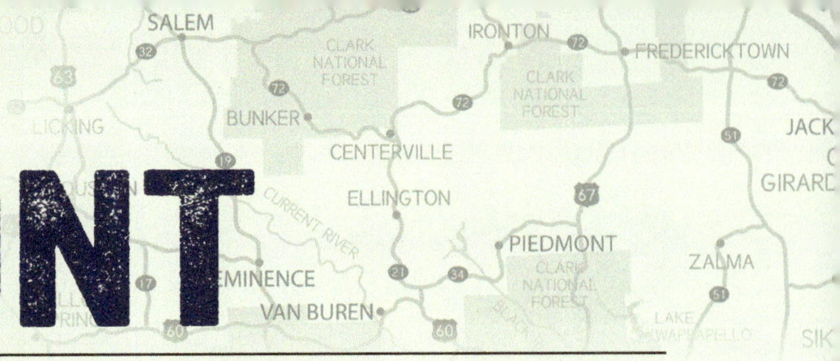

PIEDMONT

Wayne County POPULATION **1,859**

Founding Story

Piedmont's story begins between 1853 and 1856 as the homestead of two brothers, one who farmed and one who eventually opened a general store, in what was then called Danielsville. The store drew customers and eventually settlers, followed by the opening of a church, school, post office, and stagecoach line. The town continued steady growth, especially as the St. Louis, Iron Mountain, and Southern Railway was built through Piedmont, creating a stronger economic connection to bigger cities. In the 1940s and 1950s, the Clearwater Dam was constructed, drawing nationwide attention, and is considered the most significant development in Piedmont's history. Subsequently, Clearwater Lake, created by the dam, became a popular tourist attraction for its clear, spring-fed waters. It remains so to this day, drawing in people from all over during the warmer months. There are many facets to Piedmont's story, some of which are out of this world, so come prepared to explore the outdoors and learn all about what makes this place unique.

Residents and visitors alike flock to Clearwater Lake in the warmer months to cool off in one of several designated beach areas.
Courtesy of the US Army Corps of Engineers

Piedmont has a rich history that they're excited to showcase to visitors.
Courtesy of City of Piedmont

 Legends

Chester Barnett, an early Hollywood film actor with more than 175 film credits, was born in Piedmont. In addition, chemist Robert Banks, who grew up in Piedmont and attended the University of Missouri-Rolla (now Missouri University of Science and Technology), invented crystalline polypropylene and high-density polyethylene with fellow chemist Paul Hogan in 1951. These plastics have now made their way into nearly every facet of American life.

Lore

Because of a high number of reported UFO sightings, Piedmont has been named the State UFO Capital of Missouri, a title that the town celebrated by opening a park dedicated to its UFO history.

Attractions

Piedmont is known for its numerous outdoor recreation facilities and outfitters. While in Piedmont, visit Clearwater Lake and nearby Sam A. Baker State Park. Explore the beautiful Black River, and of course, immerse yourself in sci-fi at Piedmont-UFO Capital of Missouri Park.

Events

Come to Piedmont for the Wayne County Outdoor Expo, Ozark Heritage Festival, and Piedmont UFO Fest.

Vitals / Fun Facts

- Piedmont, or "foot of the mountain," gets its name for its location at the foot of Clark's Mountain about two miles north of town. Clark Mountain's summit is 1,424 feet.

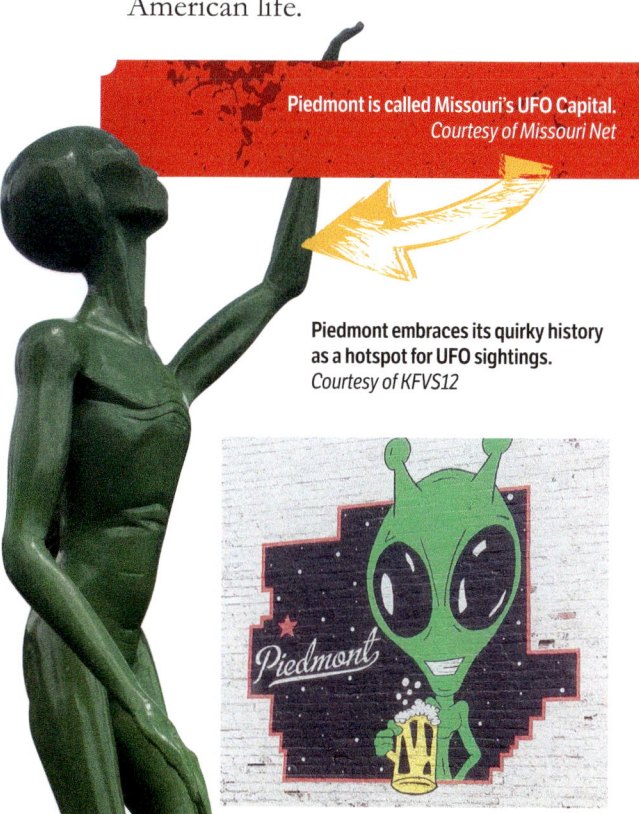

Piedmont is called Missouri's UFO Capital.
Courtesy of Missouri Net

Piedmont embraces its quirky history as a hotspot for UFO sightings.
Courtesy of KFVS12

Rocheport has repurposed historic buildings, like this bed-and-breakfast that was once the Rocheport school.
Courtesy of City of Rocheport

ROCHEPORT

Boone County
POPULATION 201

Founding Story

Rocheport is another example of a beautiful Missouri River town, with scenic overlooks and historic buildings providing a lovely backdrop for a visit. It also happens to be a community with a rich history. The area was highly desirable for its proximity to the Missouri River, its access to both salt and freshwater springs, fertile land for growing crops, and the protection of the high river bluffs. We know Lewis and Clark passed through this area in June of 1804 because it's been noted in their journals, but the town wasn't officially established until 1825.

Rocheport's beginnings mostly consisted of a trading post along the Missouri River for settlers and local Indigenous peoples. As steamboat commerce grew along the Missouri River, so did the town, which adapted to serve the needs of this up-and-coming enterprise. The Civil War was not kind to Rocheport, like many other small communities, and the town fell victim to raids from both Union and Confederate troops, including the infamous "Bloody Bill" Anderson. The town took some time to recover its population and its businesses after the war, but the building of a turnpike for stagecoaches and the starting of a bank and newspaper helped, as well as the coming of the Katy Railroad in the late 19th century.

Rocheport's growth continued into the 20th century, as the railroad grew and brought more economic potential and more people. In 1976, the entire town was placed on the National Register of Historic Places, and the Rocheport Historic Preservation Commission strives to ensure the community maintains its historic integrity and beauty.

Though once considered a dying community, when some historic homes started being rehabbed, interest in the town and its local history was soon revived. When Les Bourgeois Vineyards opened on the river bluff, providing a stunning view of the river in a beautiful winery, Rocheport became a mid-Missouri destination. The winery plus the town's history and the Katy Trail are the main drivers for Rocheport, with many businesses geared toward tourism brought in from the trail. The Katy Trail is estimated to bring over 50,000 people to the Rocheport area each year, and the community stands ready and willing to share their story, their hospitality, and their love for their town.

Rocheport is a popular place to stop along the Katy Trail and one of the most picturesque.
Courtesy of Friends of Rocheport

Les Bourgeois Vineyards is a popular spot with several different spaces to enjoy a glass and a view.
Courtesy of 417 Magazine

Rocheport makes visitors feel like they've stepped back in time.
Courtesy of Only in Your State

Legends
One of the largest steamboat owners in the West, Captain John W. Keiser, lived in Rocheport in the 1840s.

Lore
Rocheport is the home of the only tunnel on the MKT Railroad. It's not only one of the most photographed places along the Katy Trail, but the tunnel was also featured in the Stephen King film *Sometimes They Come Back*.

Attractions
Stop in Rocheport along your Katy Trail journey, or stay for a weekend. After you enjoy the outdoors, relax by wandering through the Rocheport Historical Museum. Be sure to see the Lewis and Clark replica keelboat. For a stunning view, head to the Blufftop at Rocheport (which boasts a winery, event venue, and restaurant).

The Friends of Rocheport Historical Museum is open on weekends seasonally from May through October.
Courtesy of City of Rocheport

Events

Come to Rocheport for the Rocheport Plein Air Festival and don't miss the Second Saturdays in Rocheport events, which feature live music, vendors, and food trucks in a beautiful setting.

Vitals/Fun Facts

- Lewis and Clark wrote of finding petroglyphs carved into the limestone bluffs near Rocheport. Unfortunately, the carvings are no longer visible due to their age.
- Rocheport was first meant to be called "Rockport," but the name was changed to the French style at the insistence of a French missionary in the area.
- The Whig Party held its state convention in Rocheport in 1840 and nominated William Henry Harrison for the presidency.
- One of Missouri's first rural telephone lines was built in 1878 from Columbia to Rocheport.

Rocheport is located on the banks of the Missouri River and is home to many attractions, restaurants, and more.
Courtesy of St. Louis Magazine

The only tunnel along the MKT Railroad—now the Katy Trail—is more than 120 years old and is located in Rocheport.
Courtesy of Mark S. Abein

SALEM

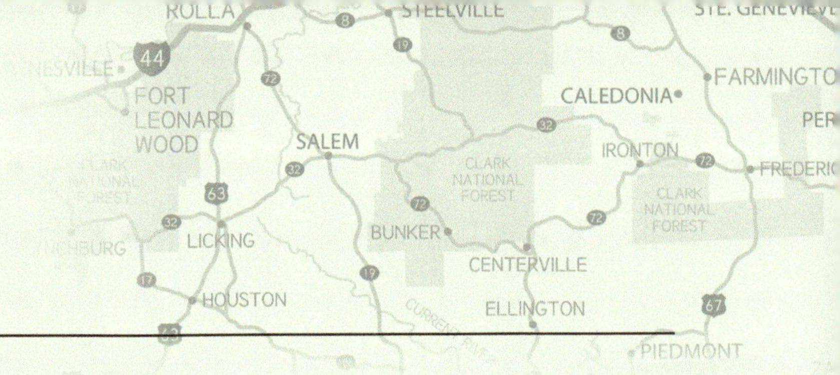

Dent County
POPULATION 4,655

Founding Story

The beauty of the Ozarks is on full display in the town of Salem. Established as a village in 1860 and formally incorporated in 1881, the town of Salem has had quite the story so far. During the Civil War, Union and Confederate troops engaged in a skirmish in Salem, with the Union claiming victory. In retaliation, Confederate troops returned and burned the county courthouse. The "Battle of Salem" was later memorialized by an artist who created a wood block rendering of the event and published it in *Leslie's Weekly*, a popular illustrated literary and news magazine. After the Civil War, the railroad's construction led Salem to be a top producer and shipper of railroad ties, using the vast resources provided by the Ozark forests. Pine was highly sought after for lumber, and oaks were processed for use in barrels, flooring, pallets, and more. In addition to logging, the community also saw success in the mining, textile, agriculture, and food service industries. Salem is regarded for its outdoor recreation, quaint downtown, and stunning Ozark landscapes, which entice visitors and residents alike.

Courtesy of 417 Magazine

The Dillards, aka the Darlings
Courtesy of City News Tribune

State Park and several conservation areas nearby, as well as the Ozark Natural and Cultural Resource Center, and the Bonebrake Center of Nature and History. Finally, don't miss the Nova Scotia Iron Works historic district.

Events

Plan your trip to Salem around any of these great events: the annual Labor Day Rodeo, the Rally America 100-Acre Wood Rally, the seasonal farmers' market, and the Christmas Parade of Lights.

Legends

The Dillards were a bluegrass band from Salem. They were best known for appearing on the *Andy Griffith Show* as the Darling family.

Salem is the hometown of award-winning author Paulette K. Jiles, whose 2016 novel *News of the World* was nominated for the National Book Award for fiction.

Vitals / Fun Facts

- The name Salem is derived from the Hebrew "shalom," meaning peace.
- Salem has been a true witness to history. Before the town was officially established, the area saw the Trail of Tears move through Missouri during the tragic period of Indian Removal. A few decades later, Salem was heavily engaged in Civil War conflict and suffered great damage.
- Nova Scotia is a nearby ghost town that is now completely overtaken by Mark Twain National Forest. The town once had the largest charcoal blast furnace as part of its iron works and is now a historic district.

Lore

Downtown Salem has a "Cursed Corner." This menacing place comprises a few square blocks of downtown Salem where a number of murders and deaths caused by freak accidents have occurred.

Attractions

While in Salem, head to the Dent County Museum or Bo's Hollow Auto Museum, and be sure to do a walking tour of the historic downtown. Salem is also a destination for those who want to commune with nature, with Montauk

Bo's Hollow features restored Ford Model As and the setting—down to the furnishings—is meant to bring you back to the 1930s.
Courtesy of 417 Magazine

Sedalia's Welcome Center at the Historic Katy Depot

SEDALIA

Pettis County
POPULATION 21,725

Founding Story

The town of Sedalia provides visitors with another example of the important role of the railroad in Missouri's story. After a neighboring town failed to secure a railroad line, Sedalia was founded by General George R. Smith in 1857 to hopefully attract the Pacific Railroad instead. He named the town after his daughter. Soon, the Missouri, Kansas, & Texas Railroad (known as the MKT or "Katy") was servicing passenger trains, the first of which departed from Sedalia in 1870. At first, the railroad line connected Sedalia to Clinton, Missouri, but crews came back in 1873 to extend the railroad from Sedalia to St. Louis. The connection helped grow Sedalia's economy and expose it to new people, ventures, and ideas.

The town's growth was strong and steady, so much so that members of the community rallied to have the Missouri state capital moved to Sedalia from Jefferson City in 1896. The effort made it to an official public vote, but Jefferson City was victorious. Moving into the 20th century, Sedalia entered a period of decline beginning with railroad strikes in the 1920s and continuing through the Great Depression, which caused the community major economic distress that they struggled to recover from. As the automobile became more popular in the 1940s and 1950s, there was less and less demand for passenger trains. In 1958, Sedalia saw its last passenger train through town.

The beautiful Katy depot building, made of red brick and limestone, stands today as a reminder of the contributions of the railroad to the town's history, and has been renovated to accommodate tourists and residents as the town's official Welcome Center, also serving as a gift shop and event venue. Today, Sedalia is a major asset to Missouri and is most known for hosting the Missouri State Fair, which draws hundreds of thousands of visitors to the area each year. During the rest of the year, Sedalia sees tourism from both the Katy Trail and from enthusiasts fascinated by Sedalia's beautiful downtown and intriguing history.

The Sedalia Katy Depot was completely restored in 2001 and now serves as a visitor center, event space, and gift shop.
Courtesy of the City of Sedalia

Scott Joplin
Courtesy of the State Historical Society of Missouri

Legends

Composer and pianist Scott Joplin lived and taught in Sedalia for some time, composing some of his best-known works here before he moved to St. Louis. Joplin's famous "Maple Leaf Rag" was published in Sedalia in 1899.

George Allison Whiteman—the namesake of Whiteman Air Force Base—lived in the area and went to school in Sedalia. Whiteman was the first US airman to die in WWII while trying to get his plane airborne during the attack on Pearl Harbor.

Lore

Sedalia was called the "Sodom and Gomorrah of the 19th century" by the *St. Louis Post-Dispatch* in 1877 because of the number of brothels, gambling halls, and saloons. The reputation lasted, with the town receiving wider attention in 1940 when *Life* magazine noted that Sedalia had "one of the midland's most notorious red-light districts." If you're interested in more of this risqué history, some of these sites still stand as historic buildings in town.

The Hotel Bothwell has been beautifully restored and maintained and provides comfort and amenities in a historic setting.

Attractions

Sedalia has a beautiful historic Katy Depot that now serves as a visitor center, event space, and gift shop along the Katy Trail. While you're exploring, check out the Daum Museum of Contemporary Art. For some historic buildings, make sure Lamy's Building, the Hotel Bothwell, the Bothwell Lodge, and the Trust Building are on your list. And of course, no visit to Sedalia is complete without a visit to the historic fairgrounds or enjoying a famous Guber Burger (first made famous at the now-gone Wheel Inn) available now at Goody's Steakburgers.

Events

Of course, the Missouri State Fair is top of the list for Sedalia events, but there's also the Scott Joplin International Ragtime Festival and the Hot Air Balloon and Kite Festival to experience throughout the year.

Vitals / Fun Facts

- The 1974 Ozark Music Festival in Sedalia was bigger than Woodstock. Yes, *the* Woodstock.
- At the height of its popularity, guests at the historic Bothwell Hotel included President Harry S. Truman, actress Bette Davis, and actor Clint Eastwood.

St. James Winery has won dozens of awards and is constantly thinking of new, innovative, and sustainable methods for winemaking.

ST. JAMES

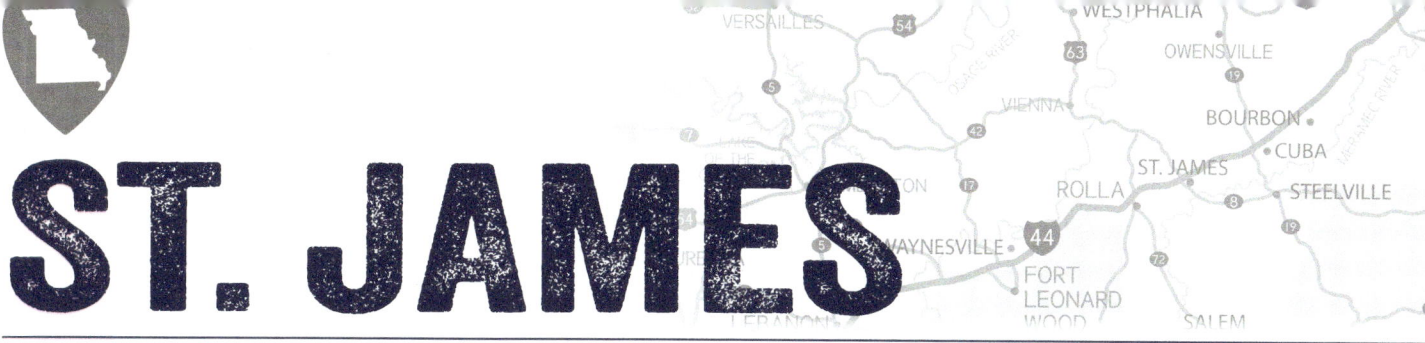

Phelps County
POPULATION
3,935

Founding Story

In Missouri, St. James is typically associated with wine, but it's not just the name of a winery! The community is rooted in rich cultural heritage and historical significance that has been preserved and celebrated in many ways throughout the town's history.

In 1826, Thomas James discovered an iron deposit in the area that eventually became St. James. James then established the first successful iron works west of the Mississippi, Maramec Iron Works, utilizing the nearby Maramec Spring for production. The area is significant to the Cherokee nation, who camped along this spring during their forced removal from their lands along the Northern Route of the Trail of Tears into the newly established "Indian Territory."

The iron from Maramec Iron Works was in high demand, which quickly grew the enterprise as their product was used by pioneers heading west, California Gold Rush hopefuls, and eventually Union gunboats that patrolled the Mississippi during the Civil War. Thomas James's son, William, established the actual town of St. James in 1859 just a few miles away along the railroad. The railroad, the iron works, and new businesses in town led to stable growth for many years, and soon Italian immigrants began settling the area and contributing to economic growth by planting vineyards and establishing wineries.

Arguably one of the most well-known wineries in the state, St. James Winery was established in 1970, and this family business has become a true Missouri mainstay and brings thousands of tourists and wine enthusiasts to the town of St. James, who can then spend time exploring all the community has to offer like restaurants, shops, and parks. The 1,800-acre Maramec Spring Park was established as a gift from Lucy Wortham James, a descendant of the town's founder, which preserved pieces of the original iron works. The park later added camping amenities and a large rainbow trout fish hatchery frequented by anglers near and far. Combined with the thriving wineries and downtown area, St. James has become a destination for tourists from all over the world.

On the grounds of Maramec Spring Park stand several historic pieces of the old Maramec Iron Works, structures that were part of the daily operations more than 100 years ago.
Courtesy of William Fischer Jr.

SMALL TOWN MISSOURI | 117

St. Jamesy Winey has been a Missouri destination for more than 50 years.

Legends

Lucy Wortham James, a descendant of Thomas James, lived in St. James. She was a philanthropist and the reason Maramec Spring Park and the historic iron works were preserved. She helped fund efforts to establish and restore some of the major components of the iron works and keep the park in pristine condition to allow for visitors to experience the natural beauty and rich history of the area.

Mayme Ousley was the first woman mayor in Missouri, elected to lead St. James in 1921 . . . just two years after women secured the right to vote!

Lore

St James went through quite a few names before being named in honor of Thomas James. The area was first called Big Prairie, and then as more settlers from Ohio came to the area, they called it Scioto after their hometown in Ohio. St. James was chosen in 1860 to honor the James family, whose Maramec Iron Works had contributed much to the area's development and success.

Maramec Spring Park combines history, nature, and recreation. Walk the trails, camp, or fish in one of the most popular places for rainbow trout in the region.

The Old Opera House been lovingly maintained to help preserve the history of the town.

Barrels at St. James Winery
Courtesy of Missouri Humanites

 ## Attractions

There is nothing in Missouri like the beauty of Maramec Spring Park. The park is renowned for trout fishing, camping, and its museums. You can also see major pieces of the original iron works that occupied the area in the late 1800s. A visit to St. James simply would not be complete without a visit to a winery. St. James Winery is an area staple, and Spencer Manor Winery is a newer establishment. If you'd like more outdoor recreation, the area is part of the Ozark National Scenic Riverways and has a plethora of beautiful areas to explore. There's also Forest City Trail for hiking and mountain biking.

 ## Events

St. James has several events that celebrate the town's history and community spirit, such as the Grape and Fall Festival, Sip n Savor event, Christmas Parade, and farmers' market.

 ## Vitals/Fun Facts

- Maramec Iron Works was the first successful iron works west of the Mississippi.
- Pieces of iron slag from the iron works (out of operation since 1891) can still be found all over Maramec Spring Park—each a true piece of history. Sometimes they are mistaken for pieces of meteorites.

Bridge over Maramec Spring

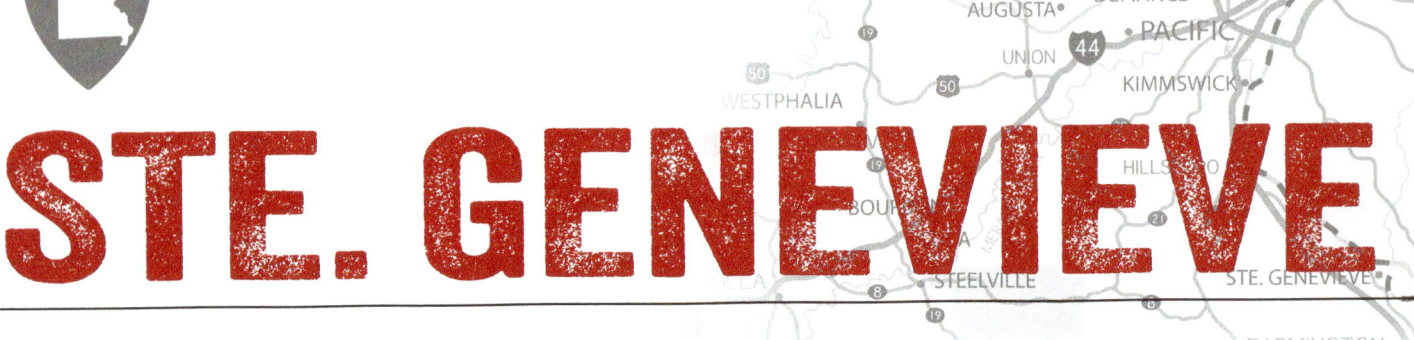

STE. GENEVIEVE

Ste. Genevieve County

POPULATION 4,999

Founding Story

It's hard to find a town whose story and buildings have been as meticulously preserved and proudly celebrated as Ste. Genevieve. Ste. Genevieve is Missouri's oldest permanent European settlement, originally founded on the banks of the Mississippi around 1735, about two miles from its current location. Flooding caused the town to move to higher ground, which is where Ste. Genevieve is located today.

Though the town was founded by French settlers, the land was ceded to Spain—along with all other French territory west of the Mississippi River—after the French and Indian War. Despite this, however, the town has retained much of the culture, language, and customs of its mother country of France, much of which is still visible to this day. Though other cities like St. Charles and St. Louis grew and prospered along the Mississippi River as well during this time, Ste Genevieve remained relatively isolated until the Louisiana Purchase of 1803.

After the Louisiana Purchase, residents of Ste. Genevieve became citizens and adjusted to this new identity as westward expansion into this new US territory brought more settlers and new endeavors to the community. New business owners built their establishments in the style of the time, which gave Ste. Genevieve an eclectic mix of both 18th- and 19th-century building styles.

The town's impeccable preservation efforts have led to the survival of many of these early buildings, and Ste. Genevieve is often regarded as one of the best living examples of 18th-century architecture. Ste. Genevieve was the location of a well-known art colony in the 1930s, which led to the community's continued connection to and love of art, which is evident throughout town. Today, the town is a popular tourist attraction for those wishing to experience a true step back in time and explore its beautiful setting, unique shops, and living history.

Ste. Genevieve Brewery is located in a historic building and provides a great setting for a pint among beautiful scenery.

Book a stay at Hotel Audubon to make your adventure in Ste. Genevieve a full weekend experience.
Courtesy of 417 Magazine

Legends

Jean Ferdinand Rozier came from France to Ste. Genevieve in the 1810s, where he lived out the rest of his life. He is most known for his partnership with naturalist John James Audubon, the namesake of the National Audubon Society.

Lore

In 1852, eight enslaved men escaped from Ste. Genevieve and fled into Illinois. They were pursued and eventually captured again, an event that would become known as the St. Genevieve Stampede. The event is referenced in historical and contemporary writings as an example of the frequency and significance of these kinds of planned escapes in pursuit of freedom.

Because of its significance, the entire town of Ste. Genevieve was named a National Historical Park.
Courtesy of the National Park Service

The Felix Valle House State Historic Site preserves an 1818 home and shares the history of the area's French heritage.
Courtesy of Great River Road

Ste. Genevieve was the first European settlement west of the Mississippi.
Courtesy of Ste. Genevieve Chamber of Commerce

Attractions

The whole town is an attraction. Ste. Genevieve is a National Historic Landmark District. While here, some highlights include the Centre for French Colonial Life, the Guibourd-Valle House, Ste. Genevieve Art Center and Museum, Ste. Genevieve Museum Learning Center, and Baetje Farms.

One of the area's top attractions is Chaumette Winery, making and sharing Missouri wine for more than 30 years.
Courtesy of Chaumette Winery

Events

In addition to the historic sites, Ste. Genevieve offers wonderful community events throughout the year, such as its French Heritage Festival, Honey Festival and Market, Jour de Fete (Missouri's largest outdoor crafts fair), and Sassafras Creek Pioneer Days.

Vitals / Fun Facts

- Ste. Genevieve has major historical significance . . . it is the first permanent European settlement west of the Mississippi
- The rich, farming-ready land that drew in Ste. Genevieve's original settlers was known as "Le Grand Champ" (the Big Field).

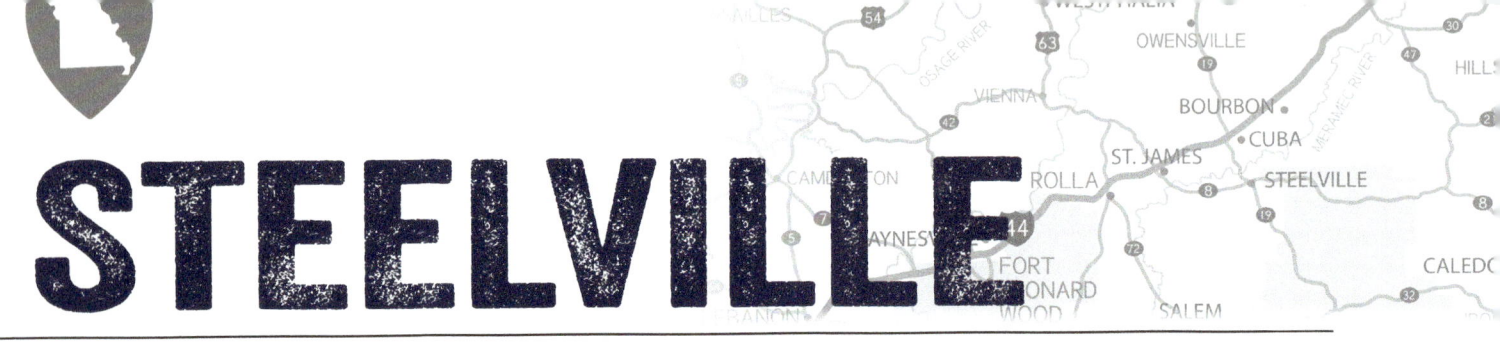

STEELVILLE

Crawford County POPULATION 1,445

Courtesy of Bass River Resort

Founding Story

Many know the Steelville area for its river recreation, as a top destination for floating in Missouri. But the town has many chapters to its story, and Steelville's multi-layered history is one of its many assets. Prior to the town's establishment, this area saw a lot of activity during the dark period of Indian Removal in the United States. Bands of Choctaw and Cherokee moved along what we now call the Trail of Tears through this area in the 1830s, and it is believed they stopped to rest, gather supplies, and bury their dead in and around Steelville. The town was laid out in 1835 and named for its founder, James Steel. The area was rich for iron mining, and the industry was so lucrative that Crawford Country started its own railroad to connect to the St. Louis and San Francisco Railway lines. While iron mining in the area has long since ended, today Steelville is a nature-lover's paradise, surrounded by lush forests, clear streams, and peaceful rivers. The community is also dedicated to preserving and interpreting Steelville's Trail of Tears history, with passionate volunteers uncovering stories and sharing opportunities for remembrance.

Legends

Nedra Sanders Broccoli was voted most beautiful brunette in the world by *Life* magazine in 1941, and she later became a model for Coca-Cola. However, she is known in Steelville as a woman who survived more tragedies than most could bear, including an almost-fatal stab wound and the death of two of her children and one of her three husbands. She eventually married Albert "Cubby" Broccoli, a film producer who went on to develop the James Bond series after Nedra died in 1958.

Steelville is known as the Floating Capital of Missouri.
Courtesy of Huzzah River Resort

Lore

Steelville has a rich history, but tragic stories as well. One of the most infamous stories from Steelville's past is the story of "Mary, a Slave." Mary was enslaved by the Brinker family on what is now the Snelson-Brinker property. Mary was hanged in 1838 for the murder of Vienna Brinker, one of the children she looked after. She was either 13 or 14 at her death, and she's considered the youngest person to be legally executed in Missouri.

Ruby's in nearby St. James, a favorite in the area for more than 50 years
Courtesy of Ruby's Ice Cream

Attractions

Popular spots in Steelville include float trips at the Huzzah Valley Resort and exploring Huzzah Conservation Area, Hoppe Spring Park, and Berryman Trail (part of the Ozark Trail). For some area history, head to Lange General Store, Dillard Mill State Historic Site, Steelville Historical Society, and Big Bend Rural School. And you simply cannot pass up a burger and milkshake at Rich's Famous Burgers, around since 1955.

Rich's Famous Burgers has been around since 1955.
Courtesy of Rich's Famous Burgers

Events

Steelville hosts concerts at Meramec Music Theatre and Wildwood Springs Lodge, as well as the annual Crawford County Fair.

Vitals / Fun Facts

- Steelville is the self-proclaimed "Floating Capital of Missouri."
- In addition to being one of the area's earliest structures, the Snelson-Brinker cabin witnessed the dark period of the Trail of Tears. The property was used as a campsite for a large group of Cherokee along the journey, and thousands of additional Cherokee and other tribes passed the property during their removal from their ancestral lands.

One of the most historically significant places in Crawford County is the Snelson-Brinker property. The cabin served as the first county courthouse, and it is also a witness to history as Native Americans camped on the property while on the Trail of Tears. Unfortunately, the cabin caught fire several years ago, but some of the structure still stands.
Courtesy of Snelson Brinker Foundation

Steelville's downtown showcases its small-town charm, friendly businesses, and historic buildings.
Courtesy of Only in Your State

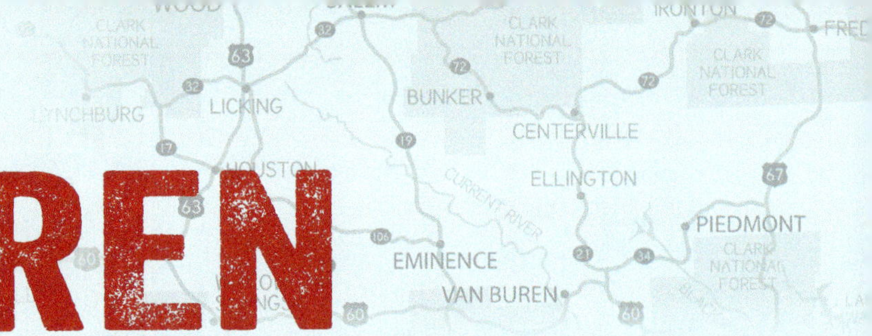

VAN BUREN

Carter County
POPULATION
747

Founding Story

Another serene Ozark community for any tourist's Missouri must-see list is the tranquil, nature-focused town of Van Buren. The community was founded in 1833 to be the county seat of Ripley County, but after more county development, it was made the seat of Carter County 12 years later and today is the largest city in the county. Situated on the Current River, the town grew due to a successful logging/milling industry, thanks to the dense pine forests of the Ozark Mountains and its location on the river for transportation. However, the demand for forestry products meant the clearing of much of the area's trees, depleting most of its resources. When the logging industry began its decline in the area, Van Buren experienced some decline. As a response to the forest depletion in their past, Van Buren has prioritized nature conservation in more recent times, with Mark Twain National Forest and Ozark National Scenic Riverways playing a large role in their efforts. Regardless of what era Van Buren finds itself in, the community has remained a beautiful Ozark town perfectly situated for the outdoor enthusiast with its proximity to state parks, national forests, and waterways.

Van Buren has several peaceful, picturesque places for spending time in nature, including Big Spring State Park and Ozark Scenic Riverways.
Courtesy of Van Buren Chamber of Commerce

Legends
Bushwackers and Jayhawkers were some of the most common outlaws in a town with a storied history of outlaw activity that could rival that of the Wild West.

Lore
In 1958, the sheriff was conducting routine patrols when he and a Highway Patrol trooper came upon a suspicious vehicle. Two men came out, were forced into the service station, and held the occupants hostage. One of the officers offered himself in place of a local woman who was in the building, and the men agreed. A multi-state crime spree ensued, with the trooper eventually being released; both criminals were convicted and sent to Alcatraz.

Attractions
While in Van Buren, visits to Big Spring State Park and the Ozark National Scenic Riverways Visitor Center are musts. Also of note are the Van Buren Riverfront Park, 21 Drive-In Theatre, Missouri Down Under Adventure Zoo, and Jolly Cone (since 1953). To outfit your float or other water adventure, head to the Landing.

Van Buren is home to one of the few remaining drive-in movie theaters in the country.
Courtesy of Visit Butler County Missouri

Events
In Van Buren, some popular events are the King of the River Bass Tournament, the Jolly Cone America Fest, the Night Sky Festival at the Ozark National Scenic Riverways Visitor Center, Riverways heritage demos, and more from Ozark National Riverways Foundation.

Vitals / Fun Facts
- The first bridge to cross the Current River—a suspension bridge—was constructed at Van Buren in 1884, but the great flood in 1904 washed it away. A new steel bridge was constructed, but flooding in 1915 destroyed that one, as well.
- Van Buren was devastated in the flooding of 2017, which took the courthouse and many businesses, churches, and homes, but the resilient community continues to rebuild.
- It is named for the eighth US president, Martin Van Buren, who was vice president when the town was founded.

Thanks to its location among springs, rivers, forests, and hills, there's no shortage of stunning views in and around Van Buren.
Courtesy of Poplar Bluff Chamber of Commerce

WAYNESVILLE

Pulaski County — POPULATION 5,432

Founding Story

Waynesville was established in 1833 and has had a post office in operation since 1834. The town served as a trading post for many years and was home to a fort built in the bluffs to protect vital supply roads during the Civil War. Into the 20th century, Route 66 came through the center of Waynesville, bringing travelers from across the country and helping Waynesville become a popular site for Route 66 enthusiasts. The town also attracts visitors because of the beautiful Roubidoux Spring, which was once a campsite and crossing along the Trail of Tears.

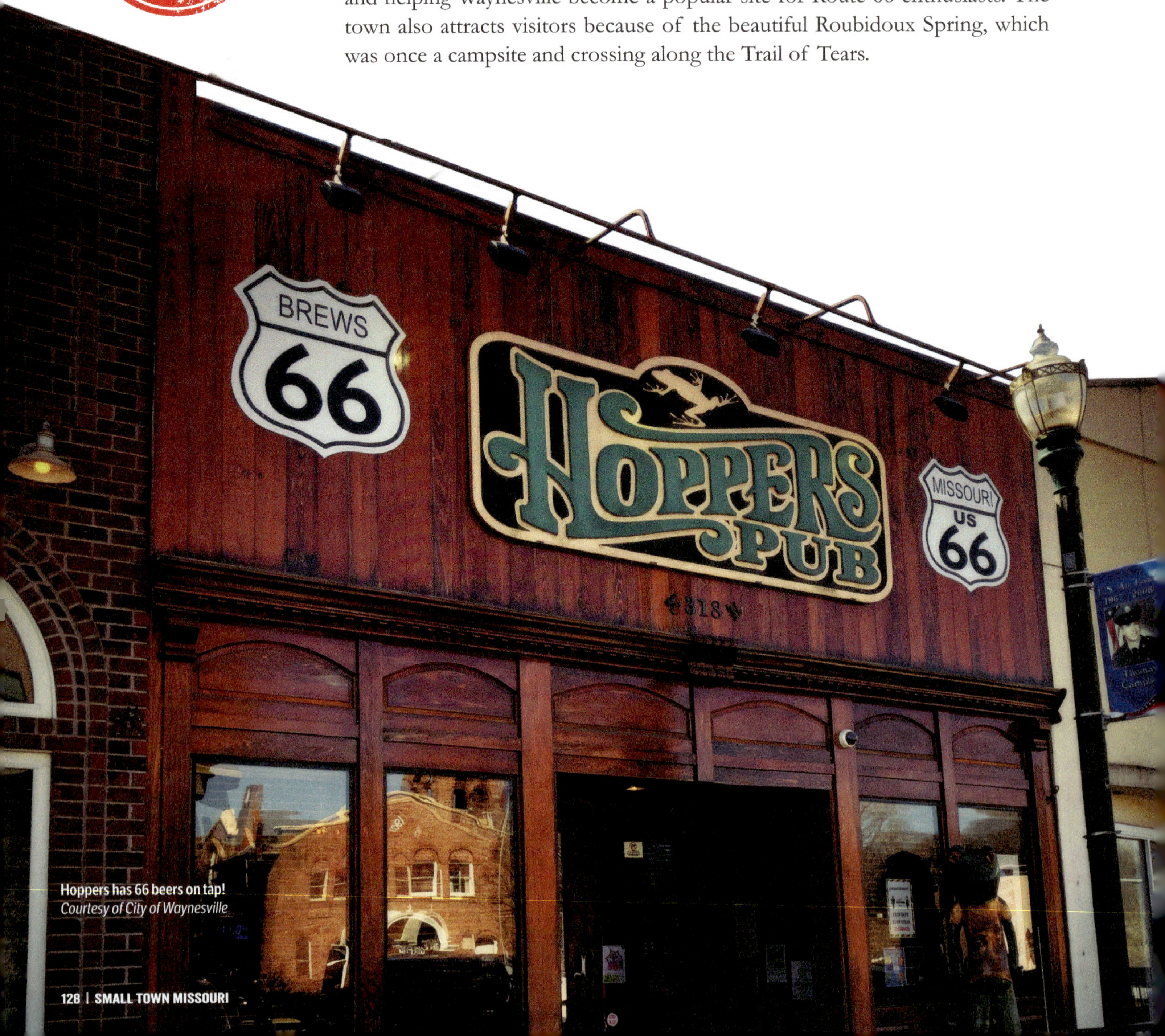

Hoppers has 66 beers on tap!
Courtesy of City of Waynesville

Legends

Juwan Morgan, an NBA forward who played for the Utah Jazz, Boston Celtics, and others, lived and went to school in Waynesville. Another professional athlete, NFL linebacker L. J. Fort, is from Waynesville and played for the Pittsburgh Steelers, Baltimore Ravens, and Philadelphia Eagles.

The Old Stagecoach Stop Museum, built in the 1850s
Courtesy of Old Stagecoach Foundation

Lore

Native American groups camped nearby at least three times between 1837 and 1839 during their forced removal along the Trail of Tears. Waynesville and Roubidoux Spring are mentioned in primary source materials from that period, including diaries of wagon masters. This history was recognized in 2005 when the area was designated as one of the only nationally certified historic sites along the Trail of Tears in Missouri.

Roubidoux Springs, a National Historic Site Along the Trail of Tears
Courtesy of Phelps County Focus

Attractions

When in Waynesville, be sure to visit Frog Rock, the 1903 Route 66 Courthouse Museum, the Old Stagecoach Stop Museum, Roubidoux Park, and Roubidoux Spring in Laughlin Park; view the Trail of Tears interpretive panels; and check out some Route 66 roadside stops.

Events

Waynesville's special events include the Route 66 Hogs & Frogs; Pulaski County Farmers' Market; children's story time and family movie nights at the Pulaski County Library; and the Cave State Cruisers Annual Car, Truck, and Motorcycle show.

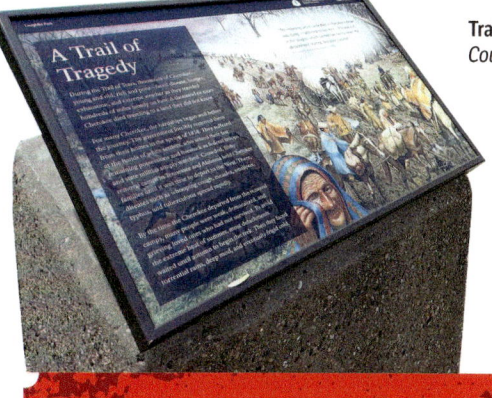
Trail of Tears Educational Panel
Courtesy of Adam Jones

Fun Facts

- It was in Waynesville that then-governor John Ashcroft signed the legislation that designated Route 66 in Missouri as a historic district. Missouri was the first state to do so.

Frog Rock is a whimsical Waynesville attraction.
Courtesy of Pulaski County Tourism

Buffalo Bill Cody
Courtesy of Buffalo Bill Cody's Yellowstone Country

WESTON

Founding Story

This area of northern Missouri was noted by Lewis and Clark for its rich soil and diverse flora and fauna, and the explorers encouraged people to experience it for themselves. The town of Weston was founded in 1837 as the first official settlement to come out of the Platte Purchase, which was a large tract of land (amounting to about six counties) ceded to Missouri by the Sauk and Fox tribes.

The first settlers of European descent in the area came from Virginia, Kentucky, Tennessee, and Louisiana, bringing with them cash crops like tobacco, which soon became the major source of income for the area farmers, followed by hemp in later years. As many of these farmers came from southern states, much of the farming was done by slave labor, a practice brought with the settlers from their original homes and not yet outlawed.

For decades, Weston was instrumental in Missouri economic vitality and westward expansion. Weston's steamboat port was located just across the river from Fort Leavenworth, Kansas, and was the fort's main marketplace. The town's location near the state border and along the Missouri River made it a pivotal location for pioneers moving west on the Oregon Trail, Sante Fe Trail, and during the California Gold Rush. It maintained its port along the Missouri river for nearly 20 years, until massive flooding moved the river and the town lost its port.

Unfortunately, that was only the beginning of a series of disasters that threatened to wipe Weston off the map, which included large fires that decimated parts of the downtown including the town's largest structure, the St. George Hotel. Throughout the years, Weston prevailed, and thanks to both public and private assistance, the St. George hotel building has been lovingly restored and welcomes visitors once more. Weston continues to be a thriving community with many attractions to meet the needs of any interest, whether it be history, arts, dining, outdoor recreation, and more.

Weston's downtown offers dining and shopping options.
Courtesy of Automotive Club of Missouri

Weston Chamber of Commerce
Courtesy of Historic Downtown Weston

The beautiful St. George Hotel dates back to 1845 and is rumored to be haunted.
Courtesy of Haunted Missouri Houses

Legends

Old West legend Buffalo Bill Cody lived in Weston with his uncle for a time after his father was attacked during an anti-slavery speech in a nearby Kansas community. His home was located on Main Street, near Short Street, and is designated with a historic marker.

Lore

During the Civil War, there were three surviving Confederates after the Bee Creek skirmish in Weston. Two were executed, and one—William Kuykendall—was spared. He went on to survive the war and moved out west, where he practiced law. He later became a judge during the first trial of Jack McCall, the man who murdered Wild Bill Hickok.

Weston Bend State Park gives visitors a beautiful setting for hiking, camping, biking, and more.
Courtesy of Missouri State Parks

Attractions

While in Weston, visit O'Malley's and sample Irish beer in the cellar of the oldest brewery west of the Hudson River, established in 1842. The McCormick Distilling Company, circa 1856, is also worth a visit, as well as the former German Lutheran Evangelical Church, which was built in 1867 and contains the cellars of the Pirtle Winery. For more history, go to the Hotel Weston, built in 1846, and the Weston Historical Museum, and be sure to visit Weston Bend State Park and the Snow Creek Ski Area (seasonally).

Events

Entertainment abounds in Weston during Weston Walking Tours, AppleFest, Wassail Festival and Market, shows at Weston Community Theatre, farmers' market (seasonal), Weston Whiskey Festival, and Historic Candlelight Homes Tour.

Vitals / Fun Facts

- In Missouri, Weston was second only to St Louis for its port and its population before it began to decline in the late 19th century.
- From fires, flooding, war, and more, Weston is known as "The Town That Refused to Die," and it almost became a ghost town before revitalization efforts began.

O'Malley's is a popular spot in Weston that is situated in stone cellars and was once home to the Weston Brewing Company (circa 1842).
Courtesy of Thinking Bigger

For seasonal fun for the whole family, check out Weston's Red Barn Farm.
Courtesy of Red Barn Farm

In addition to being a great local shopping option, the Farmer's House operates a nonprofit providing services to adults and youth with developmental disabilities.
Courtesy of Weston Chamber of Commerce

WESTPHALIA

Osage County
POPULATION
378

Founding Story

Westphalia was founded in 1835, and like many other communities in this area of the Missouri River Valley, the town was settled by German immigrants from Westphalia who named the town for their homeland. The area was perfectly situated for farming, and agriculture remains one of the top industries in the area today. Over time, Westphalia has grown into a haven for outdoor recreation, with multiple rivers, conservation areas, and trails nearby. German traditions are still alive in many of the businesses, particularly wine making, which draws visitors from all around.

Westphalia Vineyards celebrates the tradition of German winemaking, calling back to the area's heritage as a settlement for German immigrants.
Courtesy of Missouri Wines

If you're looking for time outdoors away from the winery, head to Dr. Bernard Bruns Access for fishing, boating, and hiking.
Courtesy of Missouri Department of Conservation

Legends

Westphalia is the hometown of MLB third baseman Joe Crede. Crede played for the Chicago White Sox during their 2005 World Series win, won the Silver Slugger Award in 2006, and was chosen for the All-Star Game in 2008.

Lore

A story of one of Westphalia's founders is sure to crack a smile. One of the town's most respected founders served a year and a day in a federal penitentiary for bootlegging during Prohibition. He said of his fellow Wesphalians, "I believe these are mighty fine people, even if they do make a little beer and wine on the side." How fitting that Westphalia later become renowned for its vineyards.

Attractions

St. Joseph Church is a beautiful place to visit, and no Westphalia adventure is complete without spending time at Westphalia Vineyards. For outdoor beauty, head to Painted Rock Conservation Area and Bernard Bruns Access. To learn about area history, visit the Westphalia Historical Society Museum, and for seasonal fun, go to Westphalia Trading Company.

Events

Area events include the Spring Craft & Vendor Show, regular church dinners, Christmas on Main, and seasonal festivities at Westphalia Trading Company.

Vitals / Fun Facts

- Westphalia is the oldest German Catholic settlement, with the oldest German Catholic church, west of the Mississippi.
- At Westphalia Vineyard, the wine is aged only in barrels made from Missouri oak trees.

The Westphalia Inn was built in the 1930s and is both a lodging option and a place to sample local wine.
Courtesy of Avalance Journal

SOURCES

Arrow Rock
Missouri State Parks, mostateparks.com/park/arrow-rock-state-historic-site
Advisory Council on Historic Preservation, achp.gov/preserve-america/community/arrow-rock-missouri
Village of Arrow Rock, arrowrock.org/about-discover-arrow-rock

Augusta
Town of Augusta, townofaugustamo.org/history-of-augusta-missouri
Augusta Chamber of Commerce, augusta-chamber.org/history

Bethel
Historic Bethel German Colony, historicbethel.org

Blackwater
Blackwater Preservation Society, blackwaterpreservationsociety.org/history

Boonville
City of Boonville, boonvillemo.org/history
Boonville Tourism, goboonville.com
Preserve America, achp.gov/preserve-america/community/boonville-missouri

Bourbon
Legends of America, legendsofamerica.com/bourbon-missouri
Fox 2 Now, fox2now.com/news/missouri/a-bourbon-water-tower-exploring-a-missouri-landmarks-rich-history/#:~:text=BOURBON%2C%20Mo.,that%20run%20through%20the%20area
City of Bourbon, Missouri, bourbonmo.org/about

Butler
City of Butler, Missouri, cityofbutlermo.com/1108/History-of-Butler-Missouri
Bates County Museum, batescountymuseum.org/about/#Museum_Grounds
Missouri State Parks, mostateparks.com/sites/mostateparks/files/Butler%20Report.pdf

Caledonia
Village of Caledonia, caledoniamo.org/history
Missouri State Archives, sos.mo.gov/archives/history/slogan.asp

Cameron
Cameron History, cameronhistory.com/hollywood-in-cameron.html
Cameron, Missouri Chamber, cameronmochamber.com/index.php/history
City of Cameron Missouri, cameronmo.com/261/Historic-Sites
IMDB, ibdb.com/broadway-cast-staff/dewitt-jennings-67909

Carl Junction
City of Carl Junction, carljunction.org/vnews/display.v/SEC/About%20CJ%7CHistory%20of%20Carl%20Junction
CityTownInfo.com, citytowninfo.com/places/missouri/carl-junction

Carrollton
Library of Congress, loc.gov/item/2021669607
Central Missouri Loop, centralmoloop.com/carrollton
My Hometown Carrollton, myhometowncarrollton.com
La Bella Casa Event Center, labellacasaeventcenter.com/history

Chillicothe
Visit Chillicothe, visitchillicothe.com/about-chillicothe
City of Chillicothe, chillicothecity.org/community/our-local-history-grand-river-museum
Livingston County Library, livingstoncountylibrary.org/history_1916.htm

Cuba
Visit Cuba Missouri, visitcubamo.com/how-did-cuba-get-its-name
Visit Cuba Missouri, visitcubamo.com/things-to-do
Legends of America, legendsofamerica.com/mo-cuba
Missouri Department of Natural Resources/National Register of Historic Places, mostateparks.com/sites/mostateparks/files/Historic%20and%20Architectural%20Resources%20of%20the%20City%20of%20Cuba.pdf

Defiance
Parsons House Bed and Breakfast, parsonshousebandb.com/defiance.html
St Louis Homes Magazine, stlouishomesmag.com/article/535
City of Defiance, Missouri, defiancemo.com/events
Discover St. Charles, discoverstcharles.com/plan-your-visit/about-the-area/history/daniel-boone
St Charles County, Missouri, sccmo.org/617/Broemmelsiek-Park

Doniphan
Ripley County, Missouri, ripleycountymissouri.org/history.php
City of Doniphan, Missouri, doniphan.org
K8 News, kait8.com/2023/10/27/hidden-haunts-doniphan-missouri

Eminence
EMissourian, emissourian.com/blogs/taste_of_travel/eminence-150-years-and-counting/article_84ba873c-65da-11e8-bba0-5b3254d9a693.html
KRCU, krcu.org/education/2022-04-27/abandoned-county-seat-of-shannon-county-old-eminence
HMDB, hmdb.org/m.asp?m=35926 bluegrasstoday.com/mitch-jayne-passes

Excelsior Springs
Advisory Council on Historic Preservation, achp.gov/preserve-america/community/excelsior-springs-missouri#:~:text=Excelsior%20Springs%2C%20Missouri%2C%20(population,greatest%20group%20of%20mineral%20waters
Visit Excelsior Springs, visitexcelsior.com/excelsior-history/visitexcelsior.com/bbq-fly-in-on-the-river

Fulton
Kingdom of Callaway Historical Society, callawaymohistory.org/fulton
Visit Fulton, visitfulton.com/calendar-of-events?loxi_pathname=%2Flist%2Ffuture%2F7
Art21, art21.org/artist/nick-cave

Glasgow
City of Glasgow, glasgowmo.com/?page_id=19
Missouri Life, missourilife.com/glasgow-scrappy-river-town
Visit Glasgow Missouri, visitglasgowmo.org/events-local
Lewis Library of Glasgow, lewislibraryofglasgow.org
Central Methodist University Special Collections, cmuspecialcollections.omeka.net/exhibits/show/morrison-observatory/history

Hamilton
Caldwell County, Missouri, caldwellco.missouri.org/hamilton-history/#:~:text=HAMILTON%20which%20is%20the%20largest,town%20are%20visible%20yet%20today
Hamilton Area Chamber of Commerce, hamiltonareachamber.com/hamilton-history
Missouri Star Quilt Company, blog.missouriquiltco.com/quilt-town-u-s-a-a-history-of-hamilton-missouri

Hannibal
City of Hannibal, hannibal-mo.gov/about, hannibalhistorymuseum.com/p/blog-page.html
Hannibal Courier Post, hannibal.net/news/lovers-leap-in-hannibal-to-become-a-feature-movie/article_80dd293a-fd5c-11ec-8354-5fe059c964e7.html

Hannibal Convention and Visitors Bureau, visitannibal.com/events/?utm_source=google&utm_medium=ppc&utm_campaign=madden%20semc-mo24&gad_source=1&gclid=CjwKCAjw17qvBhBrEiwA1rU9wxtSNPkPzLojO4TqsSCSw3yykcpLjirEl6ATcYWLo2tU6Kj6mXOZqRoCkuoQAvD_BwE, visitannibal.com/8-random-unexpected-things-youll-find-in-hannibal

Hermann
Visit Hermann, visithermann.com/get-inspired/hermann-history
Columbia Daily Tribune, columbiatribune.com/story/entertainment/human-interest/2013/02/17/175-years-later-hermann-is/21665843007

Jackson
Southeast Missourian, semissourian.com/blogs/fromthemorgue/entry/621944
Jackson Tourism, gojacksonmo.com
City of Jackson, Missouri, jacksonmo.org/184/Community-Profile
Missouri State Parks, mostateparks.com/sites/mostateparks/files/Jackson%20Report.pdf

Jamesport
New York Times, nytimes.com/2003/05/31/arts/martha-scott-original-emily-in-our-town-dies-at-88.html
Missouri Genealogy, missourigenealogy.org/daviess/jamesport.htm
Jamesport Community Association, jamesportmissouri.net/home.html
Missouri Life, missourilife.com/discovering-amish-country

Keytesville
Friends of Keytesville, Inc., keytesvillemo.com/history-of-keytesville
Office of the Joint Chiefs of Staff, jcs.mil/About/The-Joint-Staff/Chairman/General-Maxwell-Davenport-Taylor
Central Missouri Loop, centralmoloop.com/keytesville

Kimmswick
The Blue Owl Restaurant and Bakery, theblueowl.com/historic-kimmswick
Missouri Life, missourilife.com/quaint-kimmswick
Go Kimmswick, gokimmswick.com/about-kimmswick
Missouri State Parks, mostateparks.com/page/54983/historic-site-history

Kirksville
Kirksville Chamber of Commerce, kirksvillechamber.com/history
Visit Kirksville, visitkirksville.com/t/history-heritage
Only in Your State, onlyinyourstate.com/missouri/kirksville-devils-chair-mo
Turner Classic Movies, tcm.com/tcmdb/person/146420%7C60656/Geraldine-Page#biography
Missouri Life, missourilife.com/missouris-north-star

Lamar
City of Lamar, cityoflamar.org/196/History
Barton County Chamber of Commerce, bartoncounty.com/fallfest
University of Central Missouri (History Program), historicmissouri.org/items/show/182
Our Little Town, lamarmo.com/lamarinfo.htm

Lexington
University of Missouri Extension, extension.missouri.edu/publications/ued6053
City of Lexington, Missouri, lexingtonmo.com/default.aspx
Lexington Tourism Bureau, visitlexingtonmo.com/events
University of Central Missouri (History Program), historicmissouri.org/items/show/30
Plecner Lab at Harvard University, phil.share.library.harvard.edu/philsphridaypicks/2022/10/07/carl-stalling-project
IMDB, imdb.com/name/nm0006298
Daughters of the American Revolution, dar.org/national-society/historic-sites-and-properties/madonna-trail-statue-5

Louisiana
Louisiana, Missouri, Convention and Visitors Bureau, visitlouisianamo.com/about-louisiana-missouri
Missouri Life, missourilife.com/stark-bros-nursery-orchards-co
Great River Road, greatriverroad.com/louisiana
Historic Louisiana, Missouri, historic-la-mo.com/notable-families/john-brooks-henderson

Mansfield
Smithsonian Magazine, smithsonianmag.com/travel/the-15-best-small-towns-to-visit-in-2023-180982286?fbclid=IwAR0FMHb75VJfNgpv13k7Pn0vsJSEBpiWYZ2_A5voFXk_vd_mhh8KVix_jO0
City of Mansfield, Missouri, mansfieldcityhall.org/info.html
Only in Your State, onlyinyourstate.com/missouri/mansfield-mo-ingalls-wilder-literary-history
Laura Ingalls Wilder Home, lauraingallswilderhome.com/product/the-ghost-in-the-little-house-the-life-of-rose-wilder-lane-by-william-holtz

Marceline
City of Marceline, marcelinemo.us/home/history.html
Walt Disney Boyhood Home Museum, waltdisneymuseum.org/marceline#:~:text=Marceline%20was%20founded%20in%201888,the%20Walt%20Disney%20Hometown%20Museum
Downtown Marceline, downtownmarceline.org/visit/attractions

Marshfield
Webster County Historical Society, webstercountyhistory.wordpress.com/general-history
City of Marshfield, Missouri, marshfieldmo.gov/187/Annual-Events
Springfield-Greene County Library District, ozarkscivilwar.org/regions/webster

Mexico
Audrain County, Missouri, audraincounty.org/history

Neosho
Newton County Tourism, newtoncountytourism.org/index.php
Neosho Area Chamber of Commerce, neoshocc.com/explore-neosho
City of Neosho, Missouri, neoshomo.gov
Missouri State Parks, mostateparks.com/sites/mostateparks/files/HistoricResources-Neosho.pdf

New Haven
New Haven Preservation Society, newhavenpreservationsociety.org/historical-timeline-of-new-haven-mo
Downtown New Haven Inc., downtownnewhaveninc.org/events.html
Discover Lewis and Clark, lewis-clark.org/members/john-colter
New Haven Banner, newhavenbanner.com/home/drop-it-like-its-hot-sun-drop
New Haven Banner, newhavenbanner.com/home/new-havens-own-dan-terry-talks-about-his-ghost-hunting-work
City of Pacific, Missouri, pacificmissouri.com/199/History

Perryville
Perry County Heritage Tourism, visitperrycounty.com
Perry County Heritage Tourism, visitperrycounty.com/tower-rock-it-is-surrounded-by-a-raw-and-wild-beauty-by-amber-odom

Piedmont
City of Piedmont, Missouri, cityofpiedmont.com/history.html
Piedmont Area Chamber of Commerce, visitpiedmontmo.com/area-history
Piedmont Area Chamber of Commerce, visitpiedmontmo.com/events-1
Fox2Now, fox2now.com/news/missouri/piedmont-missouri-celebrates-ufo-history-with-new-park/ imdb.com/name/nm0055865/bio
Missouri University of Science and Technology, chemengacademy.mst.edu/academymembers/banksrobert

Rocheport
Advisory Council on Historic Preservation, achp.gov/preserve-america/community/rocheport-missouri#:~:text=Lewis%20and%20Clark%20traveled%20through,for%20settlers%20and%20Native%20Americans
Historical Marker Database, hmdb.org/m.asp?m=46345
Missouri Division of Tourism, visitmo.com/things-to-do/rocheport-historical-museum

Salem
City of Salem, salemmo.com/city/community/history_of_salem.php
Monroe County Community College, monroeccc.edu/one-book-one-community/2019/about-the-author
The Salem News Online, thesalemnewsonline.com/news/local_news/article_9095ad32-c6c3-11e6-aabd-b726f9b83912.html
The Salem News Online, thesalemnewsonline.com/news/local_news/article_443257b6-5367-11e2-a6b7-0019bb30f31a.html
Kiddle Encyclopedia, kids.kiddle.co/Salem,_Missouri

Sedalia
City of Sedalia, sedalia.com/connect/about/history
Legends of America, legendsofamerica.com/sedalia-missouri
Sedalia Convention and Visitors Bureau, visitsedaliamo.com/places/fairs-and-festivals/#downtown-events

St. James
Visit St. James, Missouri, visitstjamesmo.com/about-the-area, visitstjamesmo.com/event-calendar
Cherokee Nation, rtr.cherokee.org/sites-on-the-trail/maramec-spring
State Historical Society of Missouri, shsmo.org/manuscripts/ramsay/ramsay_phelps.html
Missouri Life, missourilife.com/april-5-1921
Springfield-Greene County Library, thelibrary.org/lochist/periodicals/bittersweet/wi77h.htm

Ste. Genevieve
Visit Ste. Genevieve, visitstegen.com/about-ste-gen, visitstegen.com/play/#museums
National Park Service Network to Freedom, housedivided.dickinson.edu/sites/stampedes/st-genevieve-stampede

Steelville
Steelville Tourism, steelville.info/big-bend-school, steelville.info/nedra-sanders-broccoli
Explore Steelville Missouri, exploresteelville.com
City of Steelville, Missouri, steelville.com/about-steelville

Van Buren
Van Buren Chamber of Commerce, seevanburenmo.com/about
Ozark Riverways Foundation, ozarkriverwaysfoundation.org/events

Waynesville
City of Waynesville, Missouri, waynesvillemo.org/history
Ozarks Sports Zone, ozarkssportszone.com/2019/07/11/waynesville-has-hidden-gem-in-shen-butler-lawson/#:~:text=Waynesville%2C%20Missouri%20is%20no%20stranger,running%20back%20Shen%20Butler%2DLawson.
Ozarks First, ozarksfirst.com/daybreak-on-the-road/daybreak-on-the-road-trail-of-tears-in-waynesville-missouri

Weston
Advisory Council for Historic Preservation, achp.gov/preserve-america/community/weston-missouri
Legends of America, legendsofamerica.com/mo-weston
Weston Chamber of Commerce, westonmo.com/calendar-2023#!event-list
Historical Marker Database, hmdb.org/m.asp?m=44543

Westphalia
City of Westphalia, cityofwestphaliamo.com/#:~:text=Westphalia%2C%20MO%20-%20a%20town%20platted,Germany%2C%20hence%20the%20town%27s%20name
Westphalia Historical Society, whs65085.org
Visit Osage County, visitosagecounty.com/see-eat-stay
Major League Baseball, mlb.com/player/joe-crede-150317

The spring made the area that would become St. James an ideal place to settle and set up industries such as the Maramec Iron Works.

INDEX

1820 Restaurant, 63
1903 Route 66 Courthouse Museum, 129
21 Drive-In Theatre, 127
50 Miles of Art Corridor, 53, 77
Adair County Historical Society, 69
African American Experience Museum, 5
Alley Mill, 41
Alley Spring State Park, 41
America's National Churchill Museum, 47
American Tractor Museum, 103
Amish businesses, 61
Amish creamery, 61
Amish furniture, 61
Amish greenhouses, 61
antique shops, 3, 80, 91
antique stores, 20, 61
Antique Trail, 33
Arrow Rock State Historic Site Visitor's Center, 3–4
arts district, 29
Audrain County Museum Complex, 91
August Busch Memorial Conservation Area, 35
Augusta Harmonie Verein, 7
Baetje Farms, 123
Baker Creek Heirloom Seeds, 79
Baker Creek Pioneer Village, 79
Ball Mill Resurgence Natural Area, 103
Barn Quilt Trail, 103
Bates County Museum, 19
Battle of Island Mound State Historic Site, 19
Battle of Lexington State Historic Site, 73–74
Becky Thatcher, 53
Berlin Wall, 47
Bernard Bruns Access, 135
Bethel Colony Spring Market, 9
Bethel Fiddle Camp, 9
Big Bend Rural School, 125
Big Spring State Park, 126–127
BIGFOOT 4x4, 97–99
Black River, 105
Blackburn Park, 99
blacksmith, 65
Blackwater Depot, 11
Blue Owl Restaurant and Bakery, 65
Blue Springs Creek Conservation Area, 17
Blue Springs Ranch, 17
Blufftop at Rocheport, 108
Bo's Hollow Auto Museum, 111
Bollinger Mill State Historic Site, 59
Bonebrake Center of Nature and History, 111
Boone Monument Village, 87
Boonville's Depot, 15
Bothwell Lodge, 115
Briarbrook Golf Course, 25
Broemmelsiek Park, 35
Bulldog Lake, 25
Burger Bar and Dari Maid, 27
Butler Original Generator, 19
Caledonia Historic District, 21
Cameron Cemetery Tour, 23
Cannonball at the County Courthouse, 74
Cape Girardeau Conservation Nature Center, 59

Cape Girardeau County History Center, 59
Cape Safari Park, 59
Carl Junction Access, 25
Carroll County Mercantile, 27
Carroll County Museum, 27
Cave Hollow West Winery, 53
Cedar Gap Conservation Area, 79
Cedar Gap Plateau, 79
Center Creek Park, 25
Centre for French Colonial Life, 123
Christkindl Markt, 57
Clearwater Lake, 104–105
Concert Hall and Barrel, 57
Conservation Areas, 35, 97, 111, 134
country stores, 61
Court Street, 47
Cranberry Bend National Fish and Wildlife Refuge, 27
Crawford County Historical Society Museum, 33
Crystal Lake Park, 74
Cuba Mural Trail, 33
Current River, 37, 39, 41, 126–127
Current River Heritage Museum, 39
Curtain Call Theatre, 69
Dalton Bottoms Access, 63
Daniel Boone Burial Site, 87
Daum Museum of Contemporary Art, 115
Dent County Museum, 111
Depot Museum, 23
Deutschheim State Historic Site, 56
Diamond, Missouri, 93
Dillard Mill State Historic Site, 125
eagle watching, 77
Echo Bluff State Park, 41
Elms Hotel, 43–45
Excelsior Springs, iii, 43–45
farmers market, 69
Ferry Boat Landing, 95
Forest City Trail, 119
Frog Rock, 129
General Maxwell Taylor Park, 63
George Caleb Bingham House, 5
George Washington Carver National Monument, 93
German Communities of Frohna, Altenburg, Biehle, and Brazeau, 103
German Lutheran Evangelical Church, 133
Gingerich Dutch Pantry, 61
Glasgow Lewis Library, 49
Glasgow Museum, 49
Goody's Steakburgers, 115
Grabs House, 87
Graceland, 89, 91
Grand Pass Conservation Area, 27
Grand River Historical Society Museum, 29
Green Estate Park, 91
Guibourd-Valle House, 123
Hall of Waters, 43–45
Hannibal History Museum, 53
Harry S. Truman Birthplace, 71
Heartland Farms, 17
Henderson's Drug Store, 49

Heritage Homestead, 36, 39
Hermann Wurst Haus, 56
Hidden Waters Nature Park, 83
Historic Bethel German Colony, 9
Historic Brick District, 47
Historic Cameron Walking Tour, 23
historic churches, 95
Historic Daniel Boone Home, 35
Historic District, 21, 53, 56, 73–75, 111, 129
Historic Downtown, 7, 19, 93, 111, 131
Historic Downtown Neosho Walking Tour, 93
Historic Faherty House, 103
Historic Hermann Museum, 56–57
historic homes, 18, 21, 27, 46–47, 64, 74, 107
Historic Masonic Lodge, 21
Historic Uptown Jackson, 59
Home of Sliced Bread, 29
Homestead Hearth, 91
Hoppe Spring Park, 125
Hotel Bothwell, 114–115
Hotel Weston, 133
Hubble Space Telescope, 83
Hubert Conservation Area, 63
Huzzah Conservation Area, 125
Huzzah Valley Resort, 125
Iron Horse Hotel (or Frady Hotel), 11
J. Huston Tavern, The, 3, 5
J. C. Penney Museum, 51
Jacks Fork River, 41
Jensen's Point, 99
Jim's Journey: The Huck Finn Freedom Center, 53
John Colter Museum, 95
Jolly Cone, 127
Kate's Hallmark Shop, 91
Katy Depot, 14, 112–113, 115
Katy Trail, 7, 13–15, 34–35, 85, 87, 107–109, 113, 115
Kirksville Art Walk, 69
Kirksville Historic Site audio tour, 69
Kiwanis Farmers Market, 69
Klondike Park, 7, 35
Knowlan Family Farm, 59
La Bella Casa, 27
Landing, The, 99, 127
Landing Hub, The, 99
Lamar High School Football, 71
Lamy's Building, 115
Lange General Store, 125
Laughlin Park, 129
Laura Ingalls Wilder Historic Home, 79
Laura Ingalls Wilder-Rose Wilder Lane Museum, 79
Lewis and Clark Keelboat, 108
Lexington Historical Museum, 74
Longwell Museum at Crowder College, 93
Louisiana Area Historical Museum, 77
Lovers Leap, 53
Lutheran Heritage Center, 103
Lyceum Theatre, 2, 5
Ma Vic's Corner Café, 81
Maifest, 57

Maintz Wildlife Preserve, 59
Maple Avenue Historic District, 53
Maramec Iron Works, 117–119
Maramec Spring Park, 117–119
Marceline Carnegie Library, 81
Mark Twain Boyhood Home and Museum, 53
Mark Twain Cave, 53
Mastodon State Park, 65, 67
McCorkle Park, 22–23
McCormick Distilling Company, 133
Millionaire's Row, 53
Mississippi River, 57–58, 65, 67, 76–77, 102, 120
Missouri Down Under Adventure Zoo, 127
Missouri Military Academy, 89, 91
Missouri Quilt Museum, 50–51
Missouri Star Quilt Company, 50–51
Missouri State Fair, 113, 115
Missouri Walk of Fame, 83
Mitchell Antique Motorcar Museum, 14
Molly Brown House, 53
Montauk State Park, 111
Morning Glory Farms, 11
murals, 29, 31, 33, 102–103
Museum of Osteopathic Medicine, 69
Musser Mansion, 23
Neosho National Fish Hatchery, 93
Newton County Historical Museum, 93
Nova Scotia Iron Works Historic District, 111
O'Malley's Pub, 133
Oktoberfest, 57, 59
Old Appleton, 103
Old Courthouse, Arrow Rock, 5
Old Jail and Hanging Barn, 14
Old McKendree Chapel, 58–59
Old Order Amish, 60
Old School, The, 23, 95
Old Stagecoach Stop Museum, 129
Old Village Mercantile, 21
Onondaga Cave State Park, 17
Osage Trail Legacy Monument, 33
Ozark National Scenic Riverways, 41, 119, 126–127
Ozark Natural and Cultural Resource Center, 111
Ozark Trail, 125
Pacific Palace, 99
Painted Rock Conservation Area, 135

Pancake City, 69
Park Street Historic Complex, 62–63
Pedaler's Jamboree, 15
Peers Store, 86–87
Perry County Military History Museum, 103
Perry County Museum, 103
Piedmont-UFO Capital of Missouri Park, 105
Pinckney Bend Distillery, 95
Pirtle Winery, 133
Pommer-Gentner House, 56
Prairie Lawn School Antiques, 11
Prairie State Park, 71
Price Museum, The, 63
Purina Farms, 99
quilting store, 39, 91
Rainbow Ranch, 75
Red Barn Arts and Crafts Festival, 69
Red Cedar Inn Museum and Visitor Center, 99
Rich's Famous Burgers, 125
River & Rail Coffee, 11
Riverfront District, 94–95
Riverfront Park, 74, 127
Riverside Regional Library, 59
Rocheport Historical Museum, 108
Rockcliffe Mansion, 53
Rocky River Resort, 39
Rolling Pin Bakery, 49
Root Restaurant, 7
Roubidoux Park, 129
Route 66, 16, 31–33, 82–83, 97–99, 128–129
Route 66 sites, 31, 83
Ruth Towne Museum and Visitors Center, 69
Salty Hippo, 29
Sam A. Baker State Park, 105
Saxon Lutheran Memorial, 101–103
Scenic Driving Tour, 49
School for the Deaf, 47
Shaw Nature Reserve, 99
Shrine of the Miraculous Medal, 101
Snow Creek Ski Area, 133
Spencer Manor Winery, 119
St. James Winery, 117, 119
St. Joseph Church, 135
Stark Brothers Nurseries and Orchards, 77
Ste. Genevieve Art Center and Museum, 123
Ste. Genevieve Museum Learning Center, 123

Ste. Genevieve National Historic Landmark District, 123
Steelville Historical Society, 125
Stilabower Public Observatory, 71
Stone Hill Winery, 55–57
Strehly House, 56
Stump Island, 49
Telephone Museum, 11
Thespian Hall, 13, 15
Thom Station Trail, 25
Thousand Hills State Park, 69
Trail of Tears State Park, 59
trails, 14, 18, 66–67, 73, 134
Treloar Mercantile, 87
Truman State University, 68–69
Trust Building, 115
Van Buren Riverfront Park, 127
Van Meter State Park, 27
Veterans Memorial, 23, 103
Vietnam Veterans Memorial, 103
Vilander Bluff Natural Area, 17
Wagon Wheel Motel, 33
walking tour, 23, 81, 93, 111
Walt Disney Hometown Museum, 81
Walt Disney Municipal Park, 81
Walt's Dreaming Tree and Barn, 81
Warm Springs Ranch, 14
Wax Museum, 53
Webster County Historical Museum, 83
Weldon Spring Site Interpretive Center, 35
West End Theatre, 11
Westminster College, 47
Weston Bend State Park, 132–133
Weston Historical Museum, 133
Westphalia HIstorical Society Museum, 135
Westphalia Trading Company, 135
Westphalia Vineyards, 134–135
Willow Springs Mercantile, 44
Wine Trail, 74
wineries, 6–7, 35, 53, 55-57, 67, 73, 85, 87, 95, 107–108, 117–119, 123, 133
World War I Memorial, 74
World's Largest Pecan (Brunswick), 63